Dan Colwell

JPMGUIDES

Contents

This Way Croatia

Ancient Culture, New Nation

Crescent-shaped Croatia, with one point extending eastwards and the other reaching down along the magnificent Dalmatian coast, is poised at the edge of Europe's cultural frontier with the East. Its strategic location, natural resources and rich Mediterranean beauty have attracted a potent mixture of visitors over the centuries. The Greeks came to trade and the Romans to build. Later, the Venetians colonized the land, the Turks raided it and the Habsburgs ruled it from Vienna.

They have all left their traces, be it the Ottoman-influenced love of sweet cakes and strong coffee, or the pizzas, piazzas and red-roofed houses that give the coastal towns from Rovinj to Dubrovnik their distinctively Venetian colour. The Roman legacy in Pula and Split has left some of the best-preserved ancient structures anywhere in Europe. In Zagreb, on the other hand, a visit to the Viennese opera house might be followed by schnitzel and beer at a restaurant whose Secession architecture dates from the time of the Austro-Hungarian empire.

It is a testament to the Croatians' powerful sense of their own culture that, despite these centuries of continual conquest and outside rule, a fiercely independent Croatian identity managed to emerge and flourish. The Croatians have always seen themselves as different from their Orthodox Balkan neighbours, a bastion of Western European culture in the East. They follow the Roman Catholic Church, use the Latin alphabet and, as any of their marvellous churches, art galleries or museums will reveal, Croatian artists and architects were active participants in the cultural hurly-burly of the Renaissance.

However, since the time the Croats last inhabited their own separate state 900 years ago, political independence had always eluded them. It is in this light that ethnic Croats everywhere found it such a profoundly emotional moment when the country, splitting off from the Yugoslav federation, finally became an independent nation in 1991.

Incomparable Coastline

The most famous destination in Croatia is the coast. Whether you travel by road or sea along the 1,777 km (1,104 miles) of Adriatic shoreline, you are guaranteed a journey of spectacular scenery and breathtaking views. The brooding bare mountains running like a spine down the coast and the picturesque little red-roofed towns are the counterpoint to more than a thousand islands anchored just offshore in the translucent Adriatic (known in Croatia as the Jadransko more). A mere 66 of them are inhabited, which means that in spite of the inevitable popularity with tourists of both the Istrian peninsula and Dalmatia, there is a wealth of idyllic places for those who want to get away from the crowds. On the other hand, if you're seeking conviviality, dazzling medieval cities such as Dubrovnik, Split and Hvar hum with the best of modern restaurants, cinemas, bars and nightclubs. These pearls of the new Croatian Republic were a great drawing card during Yugoslavia's tourist heyday of the 1970s and 80s and are gleaming anew after the struggles of independence.

Whether you find yourself on a deserted island or in an action-packed town, life along the coast is sure to be easy—this is where the best wines in Croatia are made and the fish served freshly caught from the sea.

As if the people, the scenery, the cities, the sea, the islands and the mountains were not enough, nature has blessed the Dalmatian coast with a daily average of 12 hours of sunshine in summer, when temperatures seldom drop below 21°C (70°F). Here is all the abundance and exuberance of the Mediterranean at its best.

Land of Contrast

For a small country, with a population of 4.5 million and an area of only 56,540 sq km (21,825 sq miles), Croatia is surprisingly diverse. In a few days you could go from walking around a picturesque medieval Istrian town on the Adriatic to skiing in the snow-

capped alpine mountains of the Gorski Kotar region. Or enjoy the spectacular Lake District and waterfalls of the Plitvice before going on to the impressive museums and cosmopolitan café scene of Zagreb. From the capital, the rich valleys of the Danube basin are just a few hours away, while on the eastern border of the country is an Everglades-like swamp with Europe's largest bird sanctuary. There's even a Norwegian-type fjord just north of Rovinj! It's no exaggeration to say that Croatia is a veritable Europe in miniature.

Croatian Myths

Croatia's rugged natural beauty and remote situation on the edge of Europe has made it the stuff of legend since Homer's time. They say Odysseus, returning from the Trojan Wars, was waylaid by the nymph Calypso on the Dalmatian island of Mljet. Pula, on the Istrian peninsula, was supposedly founded by sailors from Colchis on the Black Sea, who had failed to catch Jason absconding with the Golden Fleece and hadn't the nerve to return home.

Centuries later, Croatia became the setting for medieval romance when Richard the Lion-Heart was shipwrecked off the coast of Lokrum on on his way back from the Crusades. In gratitude for being saved, or so the legend says, he paid for the construction of Dubrovnik Cathedral. To Shakespeare, Illyria, the pre-Roman name for Croatia, was the most outlandish place he could think of for the setting of *Twelfth Night* (though he probably didn't know where it really was).

Fortunately, Croatia's magical scenery and legendary hospitality are unquestionably real, as you'll confirm when you have made the rounds in this country still largely waiting to be rediscovered.

Flashback

The Earliest Inhabitants

Archaeological remains show that the whole Balkan region was inhabited long before the Neolithic period, 10,000 years ago. Sometime during the Bronze and Iron Ages, Illyrian tribes settled here from the east.

Increasingly secluded from their Thracian kinsmen in northern Greece, the Illyrians settled into a life of inter-tribal warfare and piracy at sea. This ultimately led to their downfall. They harassed the Greek trading posts set up on the Dalmatian islands during the 4th century BC, and to their cost, threatened Roman trade a century later. The Roman response was war, and Illyria was annexed to the Roman Empire after 229 BC.

The Roman Conquest

By the 1st century AD, the Romans controlled the entire Balkan region. But the Illyrians' warlike temperament served them well in the Roman Empire: they were recruited to the highest levels of the army, and at least five Illyrians rose to be emperor. One of

Elaborate capital in Dubrovnik's elegant Rector's Palace.

them, Diocletian, built a palace on the Dalmatian coast in the 4th century AD, and the city of Split expanded around it. In 395, in the face of threats from barbarian tribes, the Roman Empire was divided in two, with the dividing line running north-south through the Balkans. Byzantium (present-day Istanbul) was named capital of the eastern part, while the western area, including modern-day Croatia, remained under Rome.

Arrival of the Croats

Splitting the empire didn't stop the barbarians for long, and with Rome's collapse in the 5th century, Avars, Goths and Huns swept into the region. Of more lasting importance, though, was the migration to the Balkans of Slav tribes from southern Poland in the 6th and 7th centuries. These peoples, unlike the barbarians, intended to stay. One of the tribes, the Croats, colonized two provinces of the Roman Empire, Dalmatia along the Adriatic and inland Pannonia, south of the Danube. Gradually, over the next two centuries, the Croats were assimilated into the Roman church, and eventually they used the Latin script integral to it, while 7 the eastern Slavs, such as the Serbs, adopted the Byzantine Orthodox Church, the Glagolitic alphabet *(Glagolica)* developed by saints Cyril and Methodius, and later the Cyrillic alphabet.

King Tomislav

The first king of the Croats, Tomislav (reigned 910–928), was instrumental in uniting the two wings of the country, Dalmatia and Slavonia (the former Roman Pannonia), and the Croatian state that emerged became a powerful military force in the region.

Native kings ruled Croatia until 1102, when a leadership vacuum and a perceived threat from the Orthodox Byzantine Empire led to a dynastic union of northern Croatia with Hungary.

Croatia-Hungary

Although northern Croatia maintained features of its political independence, including the Sabor (the assembly of Croatian nobles) and the Ban (viceroy), it had effectively become the junior partner in the new set-up. But even greater dangers lay just ahead. In 1242, Tatar invaders swept into Europe from Mongolia, causing devastation to Hungary and Croatia and destabilizing the area. This was followed by the rise of the Ottoman Empire (modern-day Turkey) in the east. Following the Turks' crushing of the Serbs at Kosovo in 1389, northern Croatia found it had become Hungary's frontier land. In the 16th century, northern Croatia lost part of its eastern wing to the Ottoman Empire and, with the Hungarian defeat at the Battle of Mohacs in 1526, its biggest military backer was gone as well. In desperation, the Croatians elected to the throne the Habsburgs of Austria, a mixed blessing as they would rule northern Croatia for almost another four centuries.

The Habsburgs

Under the Austrians, Croatia was reduced more than ever into a buffer zone, as the main interest of the Habsburgs was to protect Vienna from the Turks. They established the Vojna Krajina, literally, the "military frontier", ruled directly by the Habsburg war council and outside the control of the Sabor, and invited Orthodox Serbs fleeing the Turks into the Krajina area to act as a barrier. (The border was dissolved and the land returned to Croatian control only in the late 19th century.) In response to the dual pressures of the Ottoman enemy and Habsburg ally, there was a Croatian peasants' revolt in 1573. A century later, Petar Zrinski, the Ban of Croatia, led a rebellion of aristocrats against the Austrians. It failed and Zrinski was executed in 1671.

The Venetians

While Hungary was securing its control of northern Croatia, the Venetians were busy as early as the 10th century colonizing the Dalmatian coast, which, with the exception of Dubrovnik, was under their authority by 1420. Venice was supremely a commercial empire, and an independent Croatian cultural tradition survived under its rule. During this time, Dalmatia's exquisite Venetian coastal towns were built. Walled and fortified, they were defensive systems against the Turks, as well as the many pirates who sailed the Mediterranean. After the Battle of Lepanto in 1571, when the joint Spanish and Venetian navy destroyed the Turkish fleet, Venice's control of the Adriatic was largely assured.

An Independent Dubrovnik

Dubrovnik, usually known during this period by its Italian name of Ragusa, stands out as a bril-liant exception to Croatia's foreign rule. It had become a wealthy, independent city-state in the Middle Ages, and subsequently kept up a balancing act between the rival interests of Hungary, Venice, the Byzantine and, later, the Ottoman empires. However, its heyday came in the 16th and 17th centuries, when it possessed a famously grand merchant fleet and was at the centre of a Croat Renaissance that saw the production of an extensive body of art, science and literature.

Napoleon's Illyrian Dream

Dubrovnik declined as an important commercial city in the 18th century, as did Dalmatia's ruler, Venice. The final blow to their status as independent republics came with the triumph of Napoleon in central Europe. In 1797, he handed Venice to the Austrians, and seven years later, his troops marched into Dubrovnik. With his Romantic sense of his-

THE BEST-LOVED PUBLIC STATUE Croatia's greatest modern artist, Ivan Meštrović, has many fine sculptures on display around the country. But his statue of **Bishop Gregory of Nin** in Split, with its titanic stature, dramatic pose and famously polished toe, rubbed for luck by countless thousands into a shiny smoothness, has become a national icon.

tory and a tendency to see himself as a successor to the Romans, Napoleon conceived the idea of re-establishing an Illyrian province under his sway, and to this end banded together Istria, Dalmatia and Slovenia. The new republic only lasted a handful of years until his defeat at Waterloo.

Back to the Habsburgs

The Treaty of Vienna in 1815 parcelled out Dalmatia to the Habsburgs. However, the Croatians had tasted an element of self-determination, and a nationalist Illyrian movement began in the 1830s, dedicated to promoting Croatian culture and language. Its crowning moment came in 1848. The Croatians had always feared the cultural dominance of the Hungarians over them, and when Hungarian nationalists revolted, the Croatian Ban, the Illyrianist Josip Jelačić, marched his troops north to fight them on behalf of the Habsburgs. He was hoping for greater Croatian autonomy as a reward, but all he received was more control from Vienna.

By 1867 further tensions had led to another political reorganization in Vienna. In the newly constituted state of Austria-Hun-

Marshal Tito's leadership held Yugoslavia's states together.

JOSIP BROZ TITO

gary, north Croatia was placed under the rule of Hungary, while Istria and Dalmatia remained Austrian. The Croats' worst fears were realised when Hungary installed its own Ban in Zagreb, and tried to impose the use of the Hungarian language. In the face of this, Illyrianism was reborn under the influence of Bishop Josip Juraj Strossmayer as an idea called Yugoslavism, the creation of a South Slav union. Others, meanwhile, advocated total Croatian independence. Both alternatives were to have a dramatic impact on Croatia in the following century.

The Formation of Yugoslavia

As part of the Austro-Hungarian Empire, Croatia fought on the side of Germany during World War I. In 1917, Croatian Yugoslavist exiles and the Serbian government, which had fled to Corfu after its defeat by Austria-Hungary, announced their intention to found a South Slav state. When the war ended, Croatia faced dismemberment by the Allies along with the rest of Austria-Hungary, and it was largely to prevent this that the Sabor voted in December 1918 to join the Kingdom of Serbs, Croats and Slovenes. The kingdom, under Serbian King Alexander I, was soon perceived to be a vehicle for Serb expansionism.

In Croatia, the major opponent of the new state was the Croatian Peasant Party, under Stjepan Radić. Tensions came to a head in 1928 when Radić was assassinated on the floor of the parliament in Belgrade. The following year, King Alexander established a dictatorship and sought to emphasize Slav unity by giving the country the name Yugoslavia. He in turn was assassinated in 1934 by extremist Croat nationalists, the Ustachi ("Insurgents"), and the country lurched precariously towards the next great crisis.

Advent of Tito

The Germans exploited this powerful Croatian nationalism when they attacked Yugoslavia in 1941. A puppet Croatian state was set up under the Ustachi leader Ante Pavelić, initially with some public support. However, the Ustachi soon proved themselves to be as ruthless as the Nazis, and up to 450,000 Serbs, Jews, Gypsies and anti-fascist Croats were killed in concentration camps such as the notorious Jasenovac. The most effective opposition to the Ustachi and the Germans came from the Partisans, whose charismatic head, Josip Broz Tito, was himself Croatian. Their support was widely based among Croats and Serbs, and despite suffering terrible losses, they succeeded in liberating Croatia by 1944.

Tito was named as marshal of Yugoslavia in 1943, and after the war he established a republic that was both socialist and federal. However, given his constant fear of civil war between Yugoslavia's constituent republics, he made sure that the country was centrally controlled by the Communist Party. During the Cold War, Yugoslavia pioneered the policy of non-alignment with the two superpowers and sought a degree of political and economical liberalism. However, the cultural revival of the 1971 Croatian Spring already saw calls for greater autonomy from the Croats, and despite a new constitution in 1974 giving more power to the republics, the old tensions began to emerge once again.

The 1990s

After Tito's death in 1980, a collective leadership of the republics tried to fill the gap and contain the competing forces of Croat, Slovene and Serb nationalism. By the end of the 1980s, this had become impossible. In the open election of April 1990, the rightwing, nationalist Croatian Democratic Union (HDZ) under Franjo Tudjman defeated the Communists, and on June 25, 1991 he declared Croatia's independence from the Yugoslav Federation. Almost immediately, the Serb minority, fearing for their position in an independent Croatia, declared their own state in the Krajina area, where they had been located since the wars against the Turks in the 16th century. Fighting broke out between the two sides. This provided the grounds for the predominantly Serb Yugoslav People's Army to attack Croatia. Vukovar in the far east was flattened, Zagreb hit by rockets and towns along the coast shelled. The world's attention was attracted by the sustained bombing of Dubrovnik that took place in late 1991, and sanctions were placed on Serbia by the European Union. The Federal Army withdrew, and the EU, then the US, recognized Croatia in January 1992 after it had agreed to include in the constitution a section on minority rights.

Various peace agreements negotiated by the UN had already been broken, and the situation drifted through 1992 in a stalemate. From early 1993, however, the Croats pushed the Krajina Serbs back in sporadic fighting, culminating in an offensive launched on August 4, 1995 which recaptured the rebel Serbs' capital at Knin (north of Split) and routed their army. Some 150,000 Serb civilians became refugees, leaving homes and villages that were often razed by the advancing Croats. In December 1995, the Dayton Agreement was

Paved with time-worn stone slabs, Dubrovnik's main thoroughfare gleams in the setting sun.

signed by the warring parties in Paris, recognizing Croatia's international borders and acknowledging the government's responsibility to take back Serb refugees.

Croatia Today

The country's political character has changed dramatically since the death of nationalist leader Franjo Tudjman in December 1999. Elections the following year saw his HDZ party ousted from power and the formation of a centre-left government under prime minister Ivica Račan. The new government followed a far more vigorous pro-Western policy, agreeing to prosecute alleged war criminals and becoming a valued point of stability in the Balkans. When the HDZ party under Ivo Sanader returned to power at the head of a nationalist coalition after the elections of November 2003, it also committed itself to joining the EU and NATO and resolving issues with neighbouring countries over matters such as the resettlement of refugees. Croatia entered the new millennium as an independent nation for the first time in nearly a thousand years. With their remarkable history of resilience, its citizens are sure to embrace the future without losing sight of lessons that the past has to offer. 13

On the Scene

Dalmatia, with its sunny climate and glorious cities such as Split and Dubrovnik, is one of the world's most beautiful locations; the Istrian peninsula has great beaches and delightful Venetian towns. And of course, there are hundreds of unspoiled islands along the coast. But to capture the full Croatian experience, be sure to spend some time in the capital, Zagreb, a lively city of considerable charm and interest. From there, head out into the Croatian heartland: the castle-filled area of the Hrvatsko Zagorje, the lush rural valleys of Slavonia that stretch eastwards, or the rugged mountainous regions of the interior.

▰▰▰ ZAGREB

Kaptol, Gradec, Lower Town, Outside Zagreb, Croatian Hinterland

Dynamic, cosmopolitan and still small enough to be covered comfortably on foot, Zagreb is packed with a surprising number of stylish shops, first-class restaurants, pleasant squares and gardens, historic buildings, and fine museums and art galleries. There's also a flourishing café culture, bolstered by the presence of Zagreb University; dating from 1669, it's the oldest in the country. Zagreb has managed the difficult balancing act of retaining its sense of history, while also moving with the times. You can climb a medieval Croatian watchtower, relive the atmosphere of an attractive Austro-Hungarian Empire town and enjoy the buzz of a modern European capital city all within the same compact few streets.

The city descends from the slopes of Mount Medvednica to the level flood plain of the Sava River. Archaeological evidence suggests that prehistoric tribes lived here, and the Romans had a settlement in the area because of its strategic usefulness. But the

St Mark's Church: a striking landmark in Zagreb.

15

city itself dates only from 1094, when a Roman Catholic bishopric was established in what is now the cathedral district of Kaptol. A stone's throw away, the rival secular town of Gradec developed soon afterwards and the two remained separate until the 19th century, since when they've been known by the collective name of Gornji Grad, or Upper Town. Zagreb expanded rapidly towards the Sava River in the second half of the 19th century, when the Lower Town (Donji Grad) was constructed. Luckily, the city fathers were a civilized lot, and the new development was surrounded by an arc of green squares and parks nicknamed "Lenuzzi's horseshoe" after its designer. The town hasn't always been so fortunate. Beyond the Lower Town, post-1950s motorway ringroads and housing blocks sprawl for miles.

More than anything, though, Zagreb is a city best enjoyed by simply getting out onto the streets and sampling it on its own terms. Take in one of the museums in the Lower Town, shop along busy Ilica, wander around the old lanes of Gradec, join in the bustle and colour of the Dolac open-air market, then recover at a pavement café and watch Zagreb go about its business.

Kaptol

The start of any walk around Zagreb should begin at its most distinguished landmark, the great cathedral. The size and character of this building ensure that on the face of it, Kaptol retains the ancient ecclesiastical flavour of an area once populated only by cler-

SPORTING LIFE

Zagreb is Croatia's sports capital. The locals follow their teams with a passion, and it's likely you'll come across one of the many major sporting events, which will probably be shown on television at full volume in every bar or café. The two biggest football sides are Dinamo and Zagreb, who play at the Maksimir Stadium east of the city centre. Matches are usually held on Sunday afternoons. Basketball is also extremely popular, with Cibona, the highly successful local favourites, competing on Sunday evenings between October and April. More unexpected, perhaps, is the huge support for waterpolo, in which Zagreb's Mladost HL are former European champions, and handball, attracting crowds of up to 10,000 to see the Badel 1862 Zagreb team. Crowds are boisterous, the atmosphere tense, but you will always feel safe.

ics of the diocese. However, tucked behind the imposing buildings of the main roadway, the Dolac market and restaurant-crowded Tkalčićeva Street see that Kaptol caters for the needs of body and soul.

Cathedral

Originally consecrated in the 13th century, the Cathedral of the Assumption of the Blessed Virgin Mary (formerly St Stephen's) has had a violent history. The first building was wrecked by Tatar invaders in 1242, while an earthquake damaged the second one in 1880. The single tower collapsed and was replaced by the twin 105-m-high (344-ft) neo-Gothic belltowers that now dominate the skyline. Inside, the church retains its ancient appearance. The apses are early Gothic, while the nave and aisles date from the 14th and 15th centuries. Look out for the 13th-century fresco in the sacristy, the Renaissance pews and ornately carved baroque pulpit. The treasury above the sacristy has some fine religious artefacts on display, including a marvellous 11th-century *Life of Christ* carved in ivory and exquisitely embroidered church vestments from the 17th and 18th centuries.

Around the Cathedral

By the turn of the 16th century, Zagreb had become the frontline against the expanding Ottoman Empire. The cathedral was fortified in 1512, and five round towers still protect their charge. They are connected by the baroque Archbishop's Palace, which incorporates the medieval chapel of St Stephen dating from the mid-13th century. Kaptol Street itself has several fine *curias*, or small

---

TRADITIONAL DANCE

It is remarkable that in a country as new as Croatia, the ancient forms of music and dance retain a central role in the lives of the people. In a place historically racked by war, they provided an important source of cultural continuity. The most famous is the *kolo*, a lively circle dance where the fancy footwork of the dancers is matched only by the exuberance of the accompanying violinists. It dates back to long before the Croats arrived in this part of the world and was probably part of a Slavic sun-worship ritual. Dancers and musicians are usually local groups but of an impressively high standard, and performances of the *kolo* and other regional traditional folk dances can be seen around Croatia in summer. It's possible to enjoy them at a single venue, the International Folklore Festival held every July.

palaces, where the early clerics lived. The oldest, the Lector's palace at No. 17 Kaptol, dates from the end of the 15th century.

Dolac

Reached via a small alley opposite the cathedral, the busy Dolac market is a daily slice of local life, where farmers from the surrounding countryside bring their produce into the city. There are also fish and meat markets, as well as handicrafts and bric-a-brac on sale. The large spire with the green dome visible on the western side of the market is St Mary's Church, built in a mixture of Gothic and baroque styles.

Gradec

Home to craftsmen and merchants in medieval times, Gradec became a fortified royal free town after the Croatian-Hungarian King Bela IV sheltered here during the Tatar invasion of 1242. It has been the heart of Croatia's political life since the 1550s, when Zagreb was first mentioned as Croatia's capital, and contains the Sabor (parliament) and the presidential palace.

Stone Gate

Gradec can be entered from Kaptol through the dark 13th-century stone gate on Radićeva Street—part of the original town fortifications built after the Tatars had put Zagreb to the torch. Inside the gate is a popular shrine to the Virgin Mary, lined with plaques giving thanks for answered prayers. The painting of the Holy Virgin is the special object of veneration. A fire in the 18th century left all non-stone parts of the gate in ashes and the only thing to survive was the painting, a miracle that has guaranteed regular votives ever since.

St Mark's Square

Continue up Kamenita Street, past the 14th-century apothecary shop once run by Niccolo Alighieri, grandson of the Italian poet Dante, to St Mark's Square. It's hard not to feel here that you've reached the symbolic heart of the nation. In the centre of the square, St Mark's Church is instantly recognizable by its strikingly colourful roof. The two large crests, the one on the left representing Zagreb, the other Croatia's medieval independent kingdom, were painted on the roof in 1880. The church itself is far older, built in the Gothic style sometime in the early 14th century. The superb carved portal is particularly noteworthy, while inside there's a powerful sculpture of the cruci-

A 19th-century funicular provides an easy route between the Lower and Upper towns.

fixion by Croatia's outstanding modern sculptor, Ivan Meštrović.

Opposite the west portal, the pastel-coloured Banski dvori was once the residence of the Ban, the Croatian viceroy, and is now the presidential palace. Badly damaged during air-raids in 1991, this elegant building has been fully restored.

The early-20th-century neoclassical building on the east side of St Mark's is the Parliament.

Meštrović Studio

To the north of the square, along Mletačka Steet, the Meštrović Studio is a small but excellent museum dedicated to the sculptor's work, housed in two adjoining buildings where he lived for twenty years from 1922. There's an impressive range of sculptures on display, from student pieces executed when he lived in Vienna to the *Mother and Child* of 1942, left unfinished when he moved to the USA.

City Museum

A few hundred metres north on Opatička Street, the city museum occupies a large complex of ancient buildings, including an old convent and one of the 13th-century fortified towers. There are displays on the history of Zagreb from its foundation in the 11th century onwards, with models, paintings, photos and various interesting objects such as mechanical orchestras, artefacts saved from the pre-earthquake cathedral, and the silver gavel with which the Habsburg emperor Franz Josef I declared the National Theatre open in 1895.

Croatian Historical Museum

Situated in an attractive baroque palace on Matoševa Street, immediately west of St Mark's, this museum covers Croatia's history from the time of the earliest Glagolitic alphabet, the invention of St Cyril. A collection of portraits of Croatian kings, maps and military uniforms from the 18th century to World War I among many other items contribute to the overall picture of the nation's past.

Gallery of Naïve Art

The gallery contains a remarkable collection of Croatia's famous school of naïve art. These untrained peasant-painters concentrate on traditional subjects such as rural life and religion, paying little heed to conventional artistic perspective. The result is startling. Bold works such as *Deer's Wedding* and *The Woodcutters*, by Ivan Generalić, and Ivan Rabuzin's *My World* combine an unsettling strangeness with an almost mystic intensity. The gallery is located a short distance south from St Mark's Square on Cirilometodska Street.

St Catherine's Church

From the gallery, turn left and head towards St Catherine's Church, built by the Jesuits in 1632. The interior is a stunning baroque confection, where the marble splendour of the pillars and altar is but an illusion of painted wood. The whole effect conspires to make a perfect setting for summer concerts.

Nearby, the Jesuits founded the school which became Zagreb University in 1669, while to the north of the church on Jesuit Square, the old Jesuit monastery now houses major temporary art exhibitions. Outside, there's a monumental Meštrović statue of the 18th-century Croatian physicist, Ruder Bošković.

Lotrščak Tower

At the bottom of Ćirilometodska, on a terrace overlooking the Lower Town, the whitewashed Lotršćak tower dates from the mid-13th century. You can climb to the top for a marvellous 360° view of the city and its surroundings. A cannon is fired from the tower each day at noon, symbolically warning off any would-be invaders.

From Gradec to the Lower Town

Across from the tower is the Uspinjača, a funicular railway constructed in 1890, which is the

---

AHEAD BY A NECK

Unknown to many, Croatia has made an indelible mark on the world's neckware. The cravat, that indispensible accessory for aspiring artists, is actually a French pronunciation of *hravti*, the Croat word for—Croatian. No one's sure why. The most likely reason is that the scarves worn by Croat mercenaries serving in Louis XIV's army became fashionable among the French troops. The cravat now graces stylish necks around the globe, leading some to suggest that the Croatians have truly got the world by the throat.

---

effortless method of negotiating the 30-m (98-ft) hill to the Lower Town. Alternatively, you can walk along the Strossmayer Promenade for scenic views of the city. On one of the benches sits a metal sculpture of the late-19th-century Zagreb writer Anton Gustav Matoš (usually graffiti- and paint-daubed), looking out at the city he loved.

Lower Town

The construction of the Lower Town received its main stimulus from the 1880 earthquake, when a huge rebuilding programme led to the large-scale development of land outside the old city walls. In 21 contrast to Gradec, the Lower Town is a planned area of wide boulevards, open squares and parks, and huge Secession-style public buildings, most notably an impressive array of museums. It has the snappier pace appropriate to a younger part of Zagreb, with plenty of bustle around Jelačića Square, busy beer halls and the constant rumble of trams taking commuters in and out of the city.

Jelačića Square

The tram hub of Zagreb and the main meeting-place for locals, this big square just below Dolac and the Cathedral hums with life. Running along the south part of the square is Ilica, Zagreb's longest shopping street. In the centre, the equestrian statue of a heroic-looking Ban Jelačić was a gift from the Austrians after Jelačić had led a Croat army to put down the Hungarian revolution against the Habsburgs in 1848. During the Communist era, when the Ban was considered a counter-revolutionary, the statue was removed. He resumed his rightful position in 1990, although where he once brandished his sword in the direction of Hungary, he now points it towards the south.

Archaeological Museum

From the south side of Jelačića Square, Praška Street leads to the Archaeological Museum. Housed in a grand mansion of the Austro-Hungarian Empire, the museum's range goes from prehistoric artefacts to items from ancient Egypt, Rome and medieval Europe. There's also a vast collection of old coins and medals.

Gallery of Modern Art

A couple of blocks further south from the archaeological museum, the gallery will put visitors on a steep learning curve about modern Croatian art. It features a large and often interesting collection of work by Croatian artists such as Bela Csikos-Sessia, Miroslav Kraljević, Josip Račić and Vladimir Becić—most of them unknown outside their home country.

Strossmayer Gallery

In the park opposite, the Academy of Arts and Sciences showcases a gallery of European old master paintings from the 14th to 19th centuries. Though it doesn't contain their premier-league material, the gallery has works by such luminaries as El Greco, Dürer and Goya.

In the entrance hall, be sure to take a look at the Baška Slab, found on the island of Krk. The stone bears one of the earliest examples of the medieval Glagolitic language of the Croats, inscribed on it at the beginning of the 12th century.

Art Pavilion

The splendid yellow fin-de-siècle pavilion was built for the Croatian contribution to the Millennium Exhibition in Budapest, and reassembled in Zagreb in 1898. Occupying an eye-catching spot in Tomislav Square, it now hosts temporary exhibitions of contemporary art. At the other end of the square, facing the railway station, is a statue of Croatia's first king, Tomislav, mounted on horseback. The escalators in front of the nearby Esplanade Hotel lead down to Importanne, a vast new subterranean shopping centre.

Botanic Gardens

The gardens, a couple of blocks west of the Esplanade Hotel, were laid out in the 1880s. There are more than 10,000 different species of plants, two attractive ponds and an arboretum landscaped in the popular English style.

Mimara Museum

To reach the finest art gallery in Croatia, head north from the Botanic Gardens past the Art Nouveau-style National Library, taking the first or second left to Roosevelt Square. The museum is in part of a huge neo-Renaissance school building dating from 1883 and named after Zagreb art collector Ante Topić Mimara, who donated his superb collection of over 3,700 paintings, sculptures, Russian and Greek icons, glassware and Chinese art. Above all, the gallery amounts to a Who's Who of Western masters, with works by Rembrandt, Canaletto, Velasquez, Goya, Murillo, El Greco, Renoir and Manet.

Ethnographic Museum

Across busy Savska Street, the highlight of this interesting museum is a fine display of Croatian folk costumes. There are also musical instruments, ceramics, lacework and jewellery from around the country.

Croatian National Theatre

Nearby, on Marshal Tito Square, the Viennese-designed neo-baroque theatre was built in the 1890s and opened by the Austro-Hungarian emperor, Franz Josef I. It's worth going to one of the regular opera performances if only for the chance to enjoy the sumptuous gilt-and-plush decoration of the concert hall. Be sure to take a look at one of Ivan Meštrović's most powerful sculptures, *The Well of Life* (Zdenac zivota), in front of the main entrance. Outside the Zagreb University Law Faculty opposite sits another of his best-known works, a woman in Buddha-like pose (in fact, the sculptor's mother) enigmatically called *The History of the Croats* (Povijest Hrvata).

23

Arts and Crafts Museum

The lovely gabled frontage of this German-Renaissance style building faces the National Theatre. Inside are displays of 18th- and 19th-century decor, giving an idea of the elegant lifestyles of the Austro-Hungarian Empire's bourgeoisie. Collectons include Gothic and baroque sculptures from northern Croatia, Art Deco furniture, clothes, textiles and ceramics.

Outside Zagreb

The area around the capital is well worth exploring. Attractive baroque towns, Croatia's most revered medieval fortress and Mount Medvednica are all nearby. And just on the outskirts of the Upper Town and not to be missed, is Mirogoj, a remarkable necropolis that ranks with the grandest of 19th-century Europe.

Maksimir Park

East of the city, this attractively designed park was once an oak forest and hunting ground for the Zagreb bishops. In 1794 the land was donated to the public by Bishop Maksimilijan Vrhovac, becoming the first public park in southeast Europe. The Bellevue Pavilion, dating from 1843, is at the centre of the park, and apart from the lakes, lawns and sculptures, Maksimir also contains the Zagreb Zoo.

Mirogoj

Designed by Herman Bollé, the architect most responsible for the Lower Town's Secession-style appearance, this vast cemetery was opened in 1876 to the north of the city walls. The neo-Renaissance arcades just inside the great domed entrance tower are especially beautiful, while the sculptures that decorate the tombs constitute one of the most fascinating galleries of Croatian art in the country. But possibly the most intriguing thing of all about Mirogoj is that its 300,000 inhabitants include Catholics, Muslims, Jews, Orthodox Christians and atheists, an ecumenical unity that has been absent from the lives of modern Balkanites.

Medvednica

Dark, forested Mount Medvednica looms over Zagreb. Head for Sljeme, the highest peak at 1,035 m (3,395 ft). You can reach it by road or take the scenic cable-car ride. There are numerous hiking trails on the mountain, and in winter it is Croatia's most popular ski centre.

Medvedgrad Castle

Built in the mid-13th century to protect the region in case the Tatar hordes were considering coming back this way, the castle has become something of a shrine to Croatia's struggle for independence—indeed, there's a 1994 sculpture called *The Altar of the Croatian Homeland* below the south tower. Most noteworthy, however, is the small octagonal Chapel of Saints Philip and Jacob, a particularly fine example of Croatian Romanesque-Gothic architecture. From almost any point there are panoramic views of Zagreb and the surrounding mountains.

Samobor

This picturesque town, 20 km (12 miles) west of the capital, is as famous for its produce as for its scenic location at the foot of the Samobor Hills. Here you can feast on the renowned Samobor garlic sausages and mustard, delicious cakes and good local wine at any of the many excellent restaurants before exploring the town. Samobor is centred on King Tomislav Square, lined with fine 18th-century townhouses and a neoclassical town hall. There are several interesting churches, including the Gothic St Michael's, dating from the 14th century and later given a baroque facelift, and the attractive Franciscan church of St Mary's. Known as the home of Croatian mountaineering since the 1870s, the town can also boast a rare Mountaineering Museum.

PARTISAN AND PRESIDENT

The great World War II resistance leader and president of Yugoslavia for 35 years, Josip Broz Tito (1892–1980) was born into a large peasant family in Kumrovec, a village just north of Zagreb. He trained as a locksmith, but his life became the most remarkable of any Croatian of modern times. Tito fought on the side of the Austro-Hungarian Empire in 1914 and was wounded and taken prisoner by the Russians. During his imprisonment he came under the influence of Bolshevik propaganda, and in the 1930s, he was arrested several times for being a Communist. But as head of the Partisans, he could claim credit for organizing the defeat of the German Army in Yugoslavia in World War II. And as a Communist president, he rejected Stalin and moved his country away from Russia's influence to forge a new, non-aligned movement with countries such as India and Egypt. However, he was also a confirmed Yugoslavist and socialist, and as such persecuted both Croatian nationalists and the Catholic Church. Modern Croatians have mixed feelings about this charismatic figure. His childhood home is now a museum and gives a vivid picture of Tito's humble peasant origins.

Croatian Hinterland

Hrvatsko Zagorje, the Croatian hinterland, refers to the rolling hills, woodlands and peaks that reach north from Zagreb as far as the Slovenian border. A combination of undulating English countryside and Swiss Alps, the region is surprisingly beautiful, although the presence of more than fifty castles draws attention to the fact that this was once a dangerous borderland confronting the Ottoman Empire. There's plenty to see in a relatively small area; the following suggestions are representative of the most interesting sights in the Zagorje.

Novi Dvori

Originally owned by the counts Zrinski in the 17th century, and altered in 1743 to give it the appearance of a baroque mansion, the castle near Klanjec was bought by Josip Jelačić, the Ban of Croatia. His tomb, an ornate neo-Gothic chapel built in the 1850s, is located in the grounds.

Veliki Tabor

The squat, fortified castle of Veliki Tabor, approximately 40 km (25 miles) northwest of Zagreb, dates from the 15th century and is one of the best-preserved of its kind in Croatia. The castle has exhibitions of art and archaeology, and each June plays host to a fencing tournament.

Trakošćan

Undoubtedly the most eye-catching castle in the country, this is everything one expects of a medieval fortress. Emerging out of a ring of tall trees and set on top of a hill overlooking a long lake, it looks as if it had been created from the imagination of a Gothic novelist. The castle was built in the 14th century, and in 1569 was given by Emperor Maximilian II to the Drašković family, who nearly went bankrupt renovating it. A major reconstruction in 1855 in the neo-Gothic style gave it the finished-off Romantic look we see today. The interior is worth visiting, with period decoration and furniture, and a huge collection of old weapons.

Varaždin

The citizens of Varaždin are proud of the fact that their city was granted the status of royal free town in 1205 under the Croatian-Hungarian monarchy, more than 35 years before Zagreb. In the 16th century, the castle was a bastion against Turkish invasion. However, it is for its baroque architecture that Varaždin is best known today. In the 18th century the Croatian Ban moved here and it became the capital of Croatia for 20 years. A disastrous fire put an end to this brief moment of fame and glory, as the Ban returned to Zagreb and Varaždin slipped into an easy-going obscurity. There are several attractive baroque churches around town, but the nicest place to start is perhaps Tomislav Square. The outdoor cafés provide the perfect spot from which to admire the Town Hall, dating from 1523, and the delightful 18th-century houses around the square.

A short walk from here takes you to the castle. From its fortifications, now grassed over, there's a great view over the town and its church spires. The medieval fortress was turned into a baroque mansion in the 18th century and altered again in the 19th. It now houses an interesting town museum, with magistrates' maces, cannon, furniture and other artefacts from the town's history. Each September a festival of baroque music is held in the castle.

A short walk to the west, the municipal cemetery is worth a visit for its well-tended rows of conifers shaped into topiary columns, outlining the avenues of graves.

Belec

This small village on the south slopes of Mount Ivanščica has, in the Church of St Mary of the Snow, one of the most outstanding examples of baroque in the entire Balkans. The church was built in 1674 but remodelled and elaborately decorated in 1741. An unobtrusive façade gives way to a sumptuous interior in pinks and pale greens. Here, the main and side altars, filled with gilt sculptures and brilliant paintings by Ivan Ranger, function in the best baroque tradition to dazzle the senses.

Spick and span, Varaždin's castle houses a fine museum.

SLAVONIA

Osijek, Kopački Rit, Đakovo

Occupying a historically important position in the Balkans, Slavonia has always been caught in the crossfire of frontier struggles, from the Roman era, when it was called Pannonia, to the time of the Ottoman Empire. Recently, it was the much-fought-over frontline in Croatia's war of independence from Yugoslavia, and eastern Slavonia was only returned to Croatian control in January 1998.

The region is bounded by the Drava river to the north and the Sava river to the south, and blocked off in the east by the Danube. Such a preponderance of water guarantees fertile soil for agriculture and lush, green countryside, earning this area the nickname of Croatia's breadbasket. The rural character of Slavonia means it is rich in peasant traditions, with music, dance and folk costumes still very much part of the people's way of life. Rustic earthiness is also evident in the regional cuisine—roast pig, paprika-flavoured *kulen* salami, freshwater fish goulash, plum brandy and good local wines. For

Đakovo's cathedral has a wealth of detail in its architecture and interior decoration.

culture-lovers, there are fascinating baroque towns, folklore festivals, Viennese-influenced Secession architecture and a stunning wildlife reserve to enjoy.

To many Croats, then, this is *domovina*, the homeland, and for the visitor it can seem a world away from the Mediterranean life of the Dalmatian coast, or the Central European cosmopolitanism of Zagreb. A trip to Slavonia is sure to complete your picture of Croatia's intriguing culture.

Osijek

Situated on the Drava River, the largest city in Slavonia is split between the Tvrdja (fort), Gornji Grad (Upper Town—upriver fron the fort), and the commercial and residential Donji Grad, or Lower Town, to the east. This is one of the few major Croatian cities to be conquered by the Turks, who were finally expelled in 1687. Afterwards, under Austrian rule, Osijek was an important trade centre, although its heyday came at the beginning of the 20th century, when it reaped the benefits of being the chief city in the region's industrial heartland. From this period the town has inherited a wealth of striking Secession-style architecture. In the Slav kingdom formed after

World War I, Osijek became something of a backwater, and its strong cultural affinities with Austria-Hungary were loosened. But today the city is on the rise once more, and there is renewed confidence about its place in the independent Croatian republic.

Tvrdja

The slightly dilapidated condition of the old town only adds to the feeling of authenticity. This is a baroque gem, built in the 18th century inside powerful fortifications designed to resist any further encroachment by the Turks. Most of the walls have long since crumbled and the old town now sits adrift from modern Osijek. As a result, the Tvrdja gives you the chance to step back in time.

There are a couple of large churches behind the main square, a monastery and several interesting barracks once inhabited by the town's military defenders, but it is the centrepiece of Trinity Square (Trg Svetog Trojstva) that impresses. The main guardhouse with a clocktower dates from 1730, while the fine regional government building was constructed in 1737. In the middle is an intriguing plague column, put up by the townspeople in 1730 in gratitude that an epidemic had ended. The Holy Trinity tops the column while around the base stand four protecting saints. In the southeast corner of the square, the Museum of Slavonia, established in 1897, concentrates on the history and culture of the region.

Upper Town

The wide parks and boulevards of the Upper Town contribute to its pleasant sense of space. From the Trvdja, you can get to the centre via the attractive Drava River promenade or along in the opposite direction to the river, you come to the busy Europska Avenija. This has a superb row of early 20th-century Secession-style townhouses and culminates in a grand old cinema dating from 1912. At the heart of the Upper Town is Trg Ante Starčevića. Around here is a lively area of shops, restaurants and markets. But most striking of all is the elegant neo-Gothic cathedral—officially the parish church of St Peter and Paul but elevated in status by the locals because of its immense size. Built in 1849, it has a soaring red-brick spire that dominates the city skyline, while the interior is especially opulent.

Kopački Rit

Just 10 km (6 miles) or so to the northeast of Osijek, this splendid nature reserve lies at the confluence of the Drava and Danube rivers. The area is in fact a huge swamp of some 177 sq km (68 sq miles) and has much the same wild, prehistoric appearance as Florida's Everglades. The reserve is visited by 270 different bird species, including the largest population of white-tailed eagles in Europe, and deer and wild boar; there's a large zoo as well.

Đakovo

Rich farming country separates Osijek from Đakovo, about 40 km (24 miles) to the southwest. The Ottoman Empire held the town from 1536 until liberation in 1687, after which the former Ibrahim Pasha mosque was converted into the parish church. The most obvious architectural impact on Đakovo, however, was instigated by its most famous resident, Bishop Strossmayer, the man responsible for the Croatian Academy of Arts and Sciences in Zagreb. He commissioned the building of a gigantic cathedral, which took 16 years to complete after its inauguration in 1866. The result, a neo-Romanesque red-brick structure with twin 84-m-high (276-ft) towers, is now one of the most distinctive churches in the country.

Proud of its reputation as an authentic home to traditional folk culture, Đakovo holds the Đakovo Vezovi, a festival of Slavonian folklore, each July. The highlight is the display of colourful, richly embroidered costumes worn by local people. Đakovo also boasts a Lipizzaner stud farm, one of the few to breed the famous white horses used at the Spanish Riding School in Vienna.

TRAGEDY AT VUKOVAR

Vukovar was one of the most beautiful baroque towns on the Danube, developing in the 18th century around the estate of the splendid Eltz mansion. Its proximity to the Serbian border meant that Vukovar took the brunt of the Yugoslav National Army's advance in the autumn of 1991. During the siege from September to November, it was mercilessly bombarded, and the population's tenacious resistance came to symbolize Croatia's struggle for independence. Before its capture by the army, however, hundreds were killed, thousands wounded, and the entire city razed. Vukovar has been returned to Croatian rule. The ruined shell of the Eltz mansion and the destroyed city around have formed a poignant monument to the horror of war. Plans to raise the city from the ashes are underway, and some rebuilding has already begun, but it seems unlikely that Vukovar will ever regain the lost innocence of the baroque town on the Danube.

The Temple of Augustus lends a classical air to Pula's town square.

rich ornamentation made it a popular curiosity during the Renaissance, and it was sketched by Palladio and Michelangelo, as well as by the later neoclassicists such as Piranesi and Robert Adam.

Nearby, a plaque on a yellow-painted house marks the place where, in 1904–05, James Joyce taught English to Austrian naval officers. Sadly, Joyce was never able to warm to Pula's charms and saw the town as a backwater, unflatteringly calling it a "naval Siberia".

Temple of Augustus

Follow Sergijevaca towards the waterfront. At the old Roman forum, this impressive temple, built in AD 2–14 with distinctive Corinthian columns, was a focal point of the Roman town. Next to it, the remnants of a temple of Diana were incorporated into the rear of the 13th-century Gothic town hall, the political centre of medieval Pula.

Cathedral

Near the harbour, St Mary's Cathedral was built in the 1440s around the ruins of a 6th-century Byzantine basilica. The dark and capacious interior has the atmosphere of antiquity, enhanced by the use of a Roman sarcophagus for the altar.

Franciscan Church

Halfway up the hill above the forum, the Franciscan church dates from the early 14th century, and has an attractive cloister with a Roman mosaic. The interior, true to the ideas of this mendicant order, is a simple, rectangular hall. The west portal, however, is beautifully decorated with shells and vine-leaf patterns. Notice the church's external pulpit, from which sermons were given when the congregation was too large to fit inside.

Kastel

For a panoramic view of the town, climb up beyond the Franciscan church to the star-shaped Venetian citadel built in the 17th century on the site of the Roman Capitol. It now contains a small history museum focusing mainly on Pula's maritime past, with old photos of the town, models and nautical equipment. Better still, take a circuit of the castle walls, with their old cannons and 360° perspective of the city.

Brijuni Islands

An interesting trip from Pula, the Brijuni archipelago lies just off the coast. This is where President Tito had his summer residence. You can see his mansion and 45-ft yacht, and there's a museum with an exhibition of photos showing him with the rich and powerful people he entertained here. An intriguing mix of figures from the Indian Prime Minister Nehru to Richard Burton and Elizabeth Taylor numbered among his guests. The islands are now a national park, with two of them, Veli Brijun and Mali Brijun, open to visitors. They boast a huge array of exotic plants, a safari park, zoo, Roman ruins and an ethnographical museum.

THE TWO BEST ROMAN BUILDINGS The Romans made an indelible mark on Croatia, and there are some remarkable examples of their buildings still standing. The amphitheatre in **Pula**, where audiences of up to 23,000 people watched gladiatorial contests, is one of the most complete structures of its kind left in Europe. Diocletian's huge palace on the Adriatic became the old town of **Split**, where you can sit at an outdoor café surrounded by 1,700-year-old Roman columns and arches.

KVARNER GULF REGION

Opatija, Rijeka, Gorski Kotar, Krk,
Cres and Lošinj, Crikvenica, Plitvice Lakes, Rab

At the meeting point of the Istrian peninsula, the Adriatic coast and the Croatian interior (Kvarner derives from *Quarnarius*, the Latin word for "four points of the compass"), the Kvarner Gulf region encompasses a fascinating variety of landscapes. You can look out from snow-covered mountain villages to Mediterranean islands where the temperature never drops below freezing. Big cities, glamorous Riviera resorts built during the heyday of the Austro-Hungarian Empire, ancient castle towns—the medieval birthplace of Croatian culture—and rugged island idylls, all rub shoulders here. The region has been a favourite holiday spot since Roman times, but the major boost to the tourist trade came in the 19th century when direct train links were established with Vienna and Budapest. Croatia's tourist industry began soon afterwards, and the Kvarner has flourished to this day.

Opatija

Arriving at Opatija after visiting the towns of the Istrian peninsula is like crossing from medieval Italy to fin-de-siècle Austria. A host of grand hotels and luxurious villas were built in the 19th century to receive the wealthy bourgeoisie of Vienna and Budapest, and the town became a Central European alternative to the French Riviera. Famous figures such as Gustav Mahler, Chekhov, Isadora Duncan and the German Kaiser came to take in the health-giving properties of the sea air. The superb seafront promenade, extending several kilometres along the Gulf of Kvarner, is named after the Austrian Emperor Franz Josef I, who had trysts with his mistress here. Numerous restaurants and cafés, where you can sample strudel and coffee, complete the Vienna-by-the-sea experience.

Rijeka

Croatia's largest port, 13 km (8 miles) east of Opatija, was badly damaged by Allied bombing in World War II, and is now a fairly grim-faced industrial city and a hub for transport in the region, especially the big Jadrolinija ferries heading south along the coast. It has been a stronghold for Illyrians, Romans, Avars and Croatians, and was a major port for the Austro-Hungarian Em-

Plitvice lakes form a sequence of startling turquoise terraces.

43

pire. After World War I, it became the subject of considerable dispute, claimed by both Italy and Yugoslavia. The Allies settled the matter by declaring it a free city, but Mussolini took possession in 1924, calling the town Fiume. Rijeka was regained by Yugoslavia in 1945. Both the Croatian and Italian names mean "river", a reference to the River Rječina, which flows into the Adriatic here.

The Korzo

Rijeka makes up for its lack of beauty by having plenty of character. Nowhere better encapsulates this than the Korzo, a wide precinct of shops, banks and cinemas running parallel to the harbour and the perfect place for the city's large population of young people to parade up and down.

Rijeka's best-known landmark, the old City Tower, with figures of the Austrian emperors Charles VI and Leopold I over the portal, is halfway along the precinct. It is known locally as the clocktower (the clock was added in 1873). This was once the sea entrance to the city, before the land down to the present-day harbour was drained and built on. Damaged during an earthquake in 1750 and restored in an elegant baroque style, it gives access to what's left of the old town, Stari Grad.

Old Town

Once you have passed through the 1st-century arched Roman Gate on Stara Vrata, barely standing, turn right to reach the circular St Vitus's Cathedral, an impressive structure built in 1638. Inside, be sure to see the renowned Gothic crucifixion, carved in wood in the 13th century.

Museums

Leaving the old town to the north, you soon arrive at the City Museum and next door the History and Maritime Museum. The latter is in an 1890s palace, once the residence of Rijeka's Hungarian governor.

Trsat Castle

Set on the edge of a steep cliff overlooking the city, the castle was built in the 13th century, and affords spectacular views of Rijeka and the Gulf of Kvarner. For those who enjoy climbing stairs, 536 of them will get you here from the town centre. Others may prefer to take a bus.

Gorski Kotar

Beginning a mere 15 km (9 miles) north of Rijeka, this scenic alpine region is known as the Croatian Switzerland. Unlike Switzerland, however, you can enjoy views of the sea from these mountain tops, and if you time your visit for late spring, you'll be able to ski on Mount Snjeznik or Mount Veliki Risnjak and swim in the Adriatic on the same day.

Within Gorski Kotar, the Risnjak National Park is an unspoilt area of primeval pine and beech forests, alpine meadows, limestone caves, lakes and rivers, with abundant flora and fauna, including lynx, wolf, chamois, wild boar, pine marten and bear. Mountain lodges and resorts can be found at Lokve, Skrad, Vrbovsko and Delnice, from where you can go mountain climbing, hiking or skiing. A must for naturelovers, this is one of Europe's great undiscovered wildernesses.

Krk

Without a vowel to its pithy name, Krk, covering 410 sq km (158 sq miles), is the biggest Croatian island. Lying just offshore from Rijeka, it was connected to the mainland by bridge in 1980. Krk island holds a special place in Croatian culture. The Baška Inscription, one of the cornerstones of Croatian literature, was discovered here, in St Lucy's Church at Jurandvor. It dates back to 1100 and was written on a stone slab in the old Slav Glagolitic alphabet. The village of Baška at the southern end of the island is especially attractive, with picturesque scenery and good places for swimming. There are many ancient Croatian churches, and the chapel of St John (Sveti Ivan), set on a hillside, has a superb panorama of the wide bay and village.

Krk Town

Some 2,000 years ago, the Romans settled in what is now Krk town and, being people who liked their comforts, built thermal baths decorated with mosaics. The 12th-century cathedral was constructed over the baths, and the mosaics can still be seen from one of the side-chapels. Reached via a small arched passageway from the cathedral, the 10th-cen-

HOUSES MIGHT FLY

Not far from Trsat Castle is the 15th-century Church of Our Lady of Trsat. It's a popular shrine, and each year on the Feast of Assumption in August, thousands of pilgrims come here from near and far. The reason? In 1291, the legend goes, angels carrying the Virgin Mary's house from Nazareth to Loreto in Italy began to tire of their burden. Spotting this hillside, they alighted and spent three years resting before setting off on their journey again. It's one of the more unusual medieval myths, but has certainly done no harm to Rijeka's tourist trade.

tury church of St Quirinus (Sveti Kvirin) has a belltower complete with onion dome. In the Middle Ages, the area around this part of Croatia was ruled by the Frankopans, Croatian nobles from Krk who were granted a certain degree of independence from Venice and Hungary and who built great fortresses along the coast to prove it. Their indomitable castle stands at the waterfront entrance to the town, offering appropriately lofty views of the surrounding area.

Cres and Lošinj

The two islands have been part of a longstanding double act; once linked by

Baška boasts one of Krk's most spectacular views.

land, separated when the Romans built a channel between them, and now connected by bridge. They are a complete contrast to each other. A short ferry ride away from Krk, Cres, the second-largest of the Adriatic islands, is wild and barren and has fewer than 4,000 people;

Lošinj, on the other hand, is less than half its partner's size with twice the population. It's a noticeably greener, gentler place, with woodland, holiday resorts and popular beaches. Both islands are havens for wildlife. Bottlenose dolphins swim in the seas around here, while Cres is home to a colony of white-headed griffon vultures, one of the last in Europe.

Crikvenica

Just across from Krk on the mainland, Crikvenica came to prominence when, like Opatija, it found favour at the end of the 19th century as a health resort and playground for the well-to-do of the Austro-Hungarian Empire. The legacy of those opulent Habsburg days can be seen in the splendid Austrian hotels and pleasant promenades. It's still a health resort: Crikvenica specializes in thalassotherapy, based on the benefits of sea water. Modern visitors are also attracted to the long sandy beaches and the same fine climate that invigorated the pallid Viennese of the fin-de-siècle.

This popular resort town comes alive at night, when you can go from risking your fortune at the casino to sampling a variety of Balkan and Mediterranean cuisines in its excellent restaurants.

Plitvice Lakes

Croatia's Lake District is about 85 km (50 miles) inland from Senj, not far from the Bosnian border. One of the great natural wonders of Eastern Europe, the Plitvice Lakes National Park is a particular favourite with Croats, who come here to celebrate the beauty of the scenery and admire the power of nature. An 8-km (5-mile) sequence of 16 crystal-clear lakes are linked together by a multitudinous cascade of waterfalls, some of which, such as the Plitvice, Veliki and Sastavci, are especially spectacular. For maximum drama, visit in the spring, when the mountain snows melt and the torrents increase in force. There's an exhilarating walking trail on wooden boards that takes you along the rivers and around the falls. Within the National Park, hikers will also enjoy Čorkova Uvala in the northwest, the remnant of a primeval forest.

HEROES OR VILLAINS?

About 35 km (21 miles) south of Crikvenica, Senj is famous in Croatia as the military stronghold of the Uskoks, brave and daring sailors—or pirates, depending on whose side you were on—of the 16th century. The Habsburgs used them and their fleet as a frontline defence against the Turks, while the Venetians, whose ships they also attacked, considered them as little more than Austrian-sponsored muggers. A two-year war (1615–17) between the Venetians and the Austrians settled the dispute in Venice's favour: the Uskoks (whose name meant "fugitives") were resettled inland, their fleet burnt, and the mighty Nehaj fort at Senj—which you can still visit today—occupied by the Austrians.

Rab

This scenic, rocky island just south of Krk has a split personality; barren and windy to the northeast, lush and pine-forested to the southwest. It's a popular resort, with the delightful old walled town of Rab as its centrepiece, and good, sandy beaches at Kampor, Lopar and San Marino.

Rab Town

Built on a steep promontory, Rab Town was a Venetian stronghold for centuries, as the grand patrician houses and splendid Romanesque belltowers testify.

The highest of the three parallel main streets has ancient churches and a row of four belltowers that dominate the terracotta roofs of the city skyline. At the southern end, at the head of the peninsula, is the monastery and small baroque church of St Anthony of Rab. A short distance away, the early Romanesque church of St Mary the Great, with a façade of pink and white marble, was founded in 1177. There's a delightful terrace outside. The separate 27-m (89-ft) belltower is said to be the finest example of Romanesque architecture on the Adriatic: note the typical Romanesque touch with the number of windows increasing on each level. Further along, the belltower of St Andrew's Church has a carved plaque announcing that it was built in 1181, while nearby, the baby of the group is St Justine's Church, dating from the 17th century and containing a small collection of religious art. You can climb the fourth tower, near the ruins of St John's Church.

North of St John's is part of the old city wall, which gives great views of the four towers and the town. Carry on through the gate to reach the cool Komrčar Park.

THE THREE BEST NATIONAL PARKS The **Plitvice Lakes National Park** boasts an impressive 8-km (5-mile) string of 16 lakes and innumerable waterfalls and cataracts. **Paklenica**, on the southern slopes of the Velebit mountains, is known for its deep gorges and sheer 400-m (1,300-ft) cliffs. Not far from Dubrovnik, **Mljet Island** is covered in pine forests, has two saltwater lakes and, in the middle of one of them, a 12th-century Benedictine monastery now used as a hotel.

NORTHERN DALMATIAN COAST
Pag Island, Zadar, Kornati Islands, Šibenik, Trogir, Split

The stunning Dalmatian coast has always been Croatia's biggest draw. The first known inhabitants were an Illyrian tribe, the Liburnians. Their conquerors, the Romans, left major settlements along the coast at Zadar and Split, while the Venetians ruled here from 1420 to the time of Napoleon. A World War I peace treaty gave parts of the coast such as Zadar to the Italians, and it wasn't until 1947 that it passed completely to Yugoslavia. The troubles of the early 1990s saw many of the ancient cities damaged by bombs. But the area is now fully restored to its position as one of the world's most scenic spots.

The northern Dalmatian coast is blessed with a wonderful range of natural beauty and first-rate cultural experiences, from the bleak moonscape of Pag to the Roman classicism of Split, from the idyllic isolation of the Kornati Islands to the Renaissance marvels of Šibenik and Trogir. On top of this, only a short distance inland are the wild and rugged Dinaric Alps, with peaks reaching up to 1,900 m (6,200 ft).

St Simeon's Church in Zadar was a revered place of pilgrimage in medieval times.

Pag Island

On the face of it, Pag's desolate lunar landscape seems to be the sort of place that only its sheep would find hospitable. This suits the local economy, as the milk they produce goes to make Pag's most famous export, the tangy *Paški sir* cheese. There's also a long tradition of lace-making, and Pag lace is highly admired. This is an island that tourism has hardly altered, and a visit here offers the chance to experience the traditional Dalmatian way of life. The resort town of Novalja, which has Roman ruins, is the main vacation centre, with hotels, watersports facilities and some good beaches.

Pag Town

Stari Pag (Old Pag) was abandoned in the 15th century, and its inhabitants moved to Pag Town, a planned Renaissance city founded in 1443. The unfinished Bishop's Palace, Prince's Palace and the parish church (St Mary's) have been attributed to the great Croatian architect, Juraj Dalmatinac. The church is especially interesting, built in an earlier Romanesque style because the citizens insisted it should resemble their old church in Stari Pag. Above the portal is a relief of the 51

Virgin Mary protecting the local people, who are wearing contemporary island costumes.

There's a small lace museum just off the main square.

Zadar

The Illyrians first settled in Zadar in the 9th century BC, but it was the Romans and the Byzantines who really developed the town—it was the capital of Byzantine Dalmatia. Zadar's natural defences—it is situated on a narrow peninsula and bordered on three sides by water—were enhanced by massive 16th-century walls, built by the Venetians to keep out the Turks. Zadar's worst attack was to come from the air, however, when in 1943–44 Allied bombers destroyed three-quarters of the buildings. To the dismay of its citizens, Zadar was shelled again in the winter of 1991 by the National Army, damaging the cathedral and houses. But things have now returned to normal, and Zadar has reclaimed its place as one of the most intriguing towns on the Dalmatian coast.

St Donat's Church

Of Zadar's many fine churches, Sveti Donat is the most impressive. Circular in plan, it is the largest pre-Romanesque building in Croatia and was built by the Byzantines in the 9th century on the old Roman Forum. To save time and effort in quarrying for stone, much of the church was recycled from existing Roman structures in Zadar. The area around it is still scattered with poignant relics of the Forum.

St Anastasia's Cathedral

On the northwest side of the Forum, the 12th–13th century Romanesque cathedral was badly damaged in World War II. The superbly decorated façade has four storeys of blind colonnaded galleries and a Gothic rose window. In fact, it's a renovated version completed soon after the knights of the Fourth Crusade destroyed the original during the sacking of Zadar in 1202, carried out in order to pay for ships from the Venetian Doge.

Archaeological Museum

Located in a modern building opposite St Donat's, the museum has a considerable collection of Roman antiquities, as well as relics from the Liburnian period and an interesting model of the town in Roman times.

Museum of Church Art

On the other side of the street, St Mary's Church dates from 1066. Its Renaissance façade was added in the 16th century and the interior refurbished in the 18th. The belltower is the oldest in Dalmatia (1105). The adjacent convent has been converted into an excellent museum of medieval, Renaissance and baroque religious art, including sculptures, paintings, and some remarkable gold and silver reliquaries.

National Museum

Near the Port Gate on Poljana Pape Aleksandra III, in the monastery next to the 12th-century St Chrysogonus's Church (Sveti Krševan), this interesting museum has displays, paintings and models illustrating the history of Zadar and the coastal towns.

National Square

Head back to lively, café-lined Široka Street, and follow it to Trg Narodni. On the west side, the 16th-century Renaissance Guard House has recently been renovated. Opposite, the Loggia has been converted into an art gallery.

St Simeon's Church

East of Trg Narodni, this church contains the exquisitely crafted silver sarcophagus of St Simeon, dating from 1380. In medieval days it attracted pilgrims from all around Europe.

Kornati Islands

Comprised of more than a hundred islands, the Kornatis make up the largest archipelago in the Mediterranean. Most are wild, deserted slivers of windswept rock—created by God, according to legend, out of boulders left over after the creation of the world—although the uninhabited Kornat Island itself is all of 35 km (21 miles) long. The islands are truly spectacular. Humpbacked and dotted with salt lakes, they're fringed with sheer cliffs that emerge dramatically from the limpid Adriatic. Unsullied by towns or traffic, the Kornatis are the perfect place for budding Robinson Crusoes. There are two ways of staying on the islands. If you're lucky enough to have a boat, you can simply drop anchor wherever your fancy takes you; or else you can overnight at a fisherman's stone cottage, where you'll be given a fishing rod and line and left to look after yourself. Fortunately, the owners check up every couple of days and bring fresh supplies in case the fish aren't biting. In any case, you'll be rewarded with great hiking, fishing, swimming and scuba-diving, or perhaps just a spot of lazy sponge-collecting around the cove-studded coastlines.

Šibenik

Idyllically located Šibenik looks out across a picturesque lagoon towards the Kornati Islands. It was first mentioned in a royal document in 1066 and served as a fortress guarding the mouth of the Krka River on which it lies. The town flourished after the Venetians took control in 1412, and thanks to its mighty fortifications held off several attacks by the Turks. The old town is still gloriously medieval in appearance, filled with ancient churches connected by an intricate web of narrow stone-paved streets.

During the 15th and 16th centuries, the city was known as a centre of Croatian culture and scholarship, and many of the nation's most famous composers, artists, scientists and writers lived here. The 14th-century Franciscan monastery, to the south of the

---

SPOT THE DOG

Croatians say that Marco Polo really came from Dalmatia; Italians counterclaim that Dalmatian dogs originated in Italy. The fact is, although nobody knows for sure where the breed was developed—some have even suggested it was India—the Adriatic coast was their first real home. Their popularity has always been high. As coach dogs, whose job it was to trot beside a carriage and look stylish, they became the ultimate fashion accessory for the 18th-century European nobility. And today, of course, Disney has made them the most famous of Croatian exports.

---

old town, was one of the most important focal points of the Dalmatian renaissance. Today it has a large collection of valuable manuscripts from the period.

St James's Cathedral

Jutting up above the red rooftops, the magnificent Renaissance cathedral was begun in 1431 and took over a century to complete. Built entirely of stone, it has withstood the dangers of fire, flood and bombshell with ease. It is the masterpiece of Juraj Dalmatinac, a sculptor and architect from Zadar who was asked by the Šibenik authorities to take over the design of the building in 1441. The work was completed by Nikola Firentinac (Nicholas of Florence). The trefoil façade, dome and gravity-defying barrelled roof, made of huge stone slabs, are especially impressive. Most striking of all, though, is a marvellous frieze of more than 70 startlingly lifelike sculpted heads lining the outer walls of the apses.

Inside the church are some fine Gothic columns, above which can be seen Dalmatinac's trademark acanthus leaf in a double row. To the right of the choir, his tiny tetraconch baptistry, with its exquisitely sculpted stonework, is one of the highlights of Croatia's church interiors.

Ivan Meštrović's masterful statue of Dalmatinac, hammer

Skradin, the headquarters of the Krka National Park.

and chisel at the ready, stands in front of the cathedral.

The large square, Trg Republike Hrvatske, is a great spot to sit and enjoy a drink. Apart from the cathedral exterior to admire, there's also the Renaissance town hall and arcaded loggia, and the Prince's Palace, dating from the Venetian era and now the city museum.

St Anne's Fortress

North of town, the mighty fortress built in the 12th and 13th centuries still dominates ancient Šibenik's maze of houses and alleys. There's a fine view of the cathedral and surrounding bay.

Krka Falls

From Šibenik, be sure to take a trip out to these powerful waterfalls in the Krka National Park, 15 km (9 miles) upriver. Here, the Krka River comes crashing over a series of limestone barriers surrounded by lush green foliage, in a formation described as the longest travertine water chain in Europe. Near Skradinski Buk, one of the most beautiful of the falls—with the only pool where swimming is permitted—a Franciscan monastery sits on a small island. The area around here is exceptionally pretty and is always a popular place for picnickers. There is a tiny museum, and in a 55 neighbouring outhouse you can see how the resourceful inhabitants used the force of the water for milling grain, washing clothes, and cleaning carpets and fleece.

Trogir

Rising out of the sea on its own island, this magnificent little town was founded by the Greeks and built by the Croats, who sheltered King Bela IV here when he fled from the Tatars attacking Zagreb, and the Venetians, who conquered it in 1420. Connected to both the mainland and the nearby island of Čiovo by bridge, Trogir is a pocket-sized delight that you could easily pass without noticing. The maze of narrow intertwining streets, broken by steps and vaulted passages, admits no cars and instead is filled with the busy traffic of people heading to the many bars and restaurants. In the town square, meanwhile, some of Croatia's finest works of art wait to be discovered.

Trogir Cathedral

Dominating the square, the Cathedral dedicated to St Lovro was built in the early 13th century and is an exceptional achievement of the Romanesque era. The main portal, flanked by statues of Adam and Eve supported by lions, was carved in remarkable detail in 1240 and signed by Master Radovan, a local sculptor.

The interior has many fine features. The outstanding Renaissance Chapel of St John, fashioned entirely from stone by Nicholas of Florence, said to be a student of Donatello, is crammed with reliefs and sculptures. Note the pagan touch in the lower part of the chapel, where cherubim clutching torches peer out of half-open doors. There's also a beautiful pulpit supported by eight columns, a two-tier ciborium over the main altar, and some impressive artefacts in the treasury.

The campanile was built across four centuries, and each level records the change in architectural styles, going from Romanesque at the bottom through early and late Gothic, arriving at the Renaissance on the fourth storey, and topped by 17th-century statuary.

Town Square

Opposite the cathedral on the main square, the Čipiko Palace is a lavishly decorated 15th-century mansion with two triple-arched windows, one above the other. Inside is a painted wooden cockerel, taken from a Turkish ship at the Battle of Lepanto in 1571 by Alviz Čipiko, the Trogir commander. The nearby Renaissance loggia, built by Nicholas of Flo-

The house façades in Trogir are delightful in their sculpted detail.

Diocletian could step out of his basement door and into a boat.

rence in the 1470s, served as law court, prison and public forum and still has the original magistrate's bench.

Split

Split is probably the only city in the world that started as a retirement home. A common soldier turned emperor, Diocletian was the first sovereign to resign voluntarily, abdicating in AD 305. With a vast empire to choose from, he picked this splendid bay on the south side of the Split peninsula to construct his sumptuous palace. It found a new lease of life 300 years later, when the provincial centre of nearby Salo-

na was sacked by marauding Slav and Avar tribes, and refugees sought shelter in the great palace. They took over the cellars and the imperial apartments, rebuilt, settled in, and eventually spread beyond the massive outer walls.

Split has kept on expanding. Today it is a major industrial city with the largest population in Dalmatia. The best place to witness the renowned stylishness of the *Splićanin* is at one of the cafés lining the palm-shaded waterfront just outside the palace.

Diocletian's Palace

The emperor's palace now forms the extraordinary old town of

Split. Covering an area of about 27,000 sq m (almost 7 acres), it has a simple rectangular layout with main streets crossing in the centre and leading to gates in the middle of each wall. Diocletian's quarters were in the southern or seaward half; the palace staff and legionaries used to live in the northern part.

Start at the waterfront. The emperor might have admired the sea view from between the columns of a covered walkway above the entrance. Enter the palace by the southern Bronze Gate *(Mjedena vrata)*; it originally gave direct access to the sea shore which came right up to the walls. The gate leads into the basement of Diocletian's central hall; on either side are the foundations of the palace *(Podrumi)*. These deliciously cool vaulted halls used to be directly below the imperial apartments and are built on the same ground plan, giving a precise idea of their shape and size. The basement now contains the City Museum, with archaeological finds, an interactive display and exhibitions of modern art.

Along the passage you arrive at the palace's centrepiece, the Peristyle. Bordered on three sides by immense Corinthian columns, this sunken courtyard has defied time to continue its original function as an open-air festival hall and meeting place. During the Split Summer Festival, concerts and opera performances are given here. At other times it's the perfect spot to sit outside a café and contemplate the 17 centuries of history in evidence around you. Behind the stairs to the south of the Peristyle, a monumental portico leads to the circular, now domeless, vestibule, the waiting

4

THE FOUR BEST CASTLES Croatia, true to its history as a vital frontier, is filled with castles. The 14th-century **Trakošćan**, close to the Slovenian and Hungarian borders, is scenically situated overlooking a lake. The mighty castle at **Varaždin**, transformed from medieval stronghold to baroque mansion, now houses a museum. **Medvedgrad**, just north of Zagreb, protected Croatia from the Tartar invasion, becoming the "altar of the homeland". A sense of history still clings to the Uskok fortress at **Klis**, the scene of a desperate stand against the Turks in 1537.

room for visiting dignitaries wishing to meet Diocletian.

Back across the Peristyle, an alley bordered by medieval buildings leads to an ancient house of worship. Originally sacrifices to Jupiter were performed here, but early Christians turned it into a baptistry. A headless black sphinx keeps watch before the entrance.

The wide thoroughfare leading east from the Peristyle takes you to the Silver Gate *(Srebrna vrata),* the site of the colourful and lively flower market. From here, wander through the warren of medieval streets to the Golden Gate *(Zlatna vrata).* On the way there's the Gothic Papalić Palace, now the City Museum. It has a fine collection of early weapons, paintings and other local artefacts.

Cathedral

The cathedral of St Domnius was once the emperor's mausoleum, and it is ironic that the last resting place of such an avid persecutor of Christians should end up as a church. A black granite Egyptian sphinx guards the entrance, and 24 columns surround the octagonal structure dominated by its medieval tower, which is worth climbing for a marvellous view of

The outside of the cathedral, fronting onto the Peristyle, has not changed since Diocletian's time.

the old city. The carved panels representing scenes from the life of Christ on the wooden main doors, completed by Master Buvina in 1214, are a masterpiece of 13th-century art.

Inside, look up at the base of the dome, encircled by a frieze of chariots and hunting scenes, with Diocletian's head set in a round stone wreath. There's a superbly animated carving of the Flagellation on the altar of St Anastasius, made in 1448 by Juraj Dalmatinac, a stone pulpit possibly modelled on the one at Trogir, and 13th-century choir stalls.

Beyond the Palace

Outside the Golden Gate, pause to admire the epic-scale statue of Bishop Gregory of Nin—a 10th-century Croatian bishop honoured for asserting the right to say mass in Croat. The statue was sculpted by Croatia's master artist, Ivan Meštrović, in 1929.

A street along the west wall takes you to National Square *(Narodni Trg),* an early-evening meeting place for young and old. The Venetian former town hall with its three Gothic arches, on the northeast side of the square, now houses the Ethnographic Museum, displaying embroidered costumes, lacework, silver jewellery and various trades.

Going south back to the waterfront, you come to Braće Radića 61

Square, dominated by the 15th-century Hrvoje Tower, part of the fortifications the Venetians built to hold off the Turks.

Archaeological Museum

At Zrinjsko-Frankopanska 25, on the north side of Split, the Archaeological Museum has a fine exhibition of prehistoric, Hellenistic, Roman and early-Christian artefacts, mainly from nearby Salona and first put together at the beginning of the 19th century—it is Croatia's oldest museum. The detailed carvings of the 4th-century sarcophagi are especially worth seeking out, and there is an impressive collection of antique and medieval coins.

Museum of Croatian Archaeological Monuments

On on Setaliste Ivana Meštrovica, west of the city near the tip of the peninsula, is another archaeological museum featuring sculpted stone fragments such as altar partitions from medieval Croatian churches. It also displays tools, jewellery, weapons, coins and everyday items dating from the 7th to 15th centuries, retrieved from graves of warriors.

Meštrović Gallery

All around Split you'll see examples of Meštrović's monumental works, such as the statues of Bishop Gregory, St John the Baptist and the poet Marco Marulić in the middle of Braće Radića Square. The sculptor's former summer residence, a little further west along Setaliste Ivana Meštrovica is now the Meštrović Gallery displaying more of his works, not only sculpture but also oil paintings and drawings. He designed the building himself and intended it to be his retirement home, but unlike Diocletian, he spent his last days elsewhere. Disillusioned with the anti-religious communist régime after World War II, he emigrated to the United States, where he died in 1962. Down by the coast in the Kaštelet, a small 16th-century castle, you can see Meštrović's Life of Christ cycle, wood reliefs around four walls, dominated by a Crucifixion.

Marjan Hill

Split's landmark beloved of all its citizens is wooded Marjan Hill, where Diocletian once hunted. A climb up the steps near the Meštrović Museum to the terrace will reward you with views of the city and its surroundings.

Salona

Near Solin, 5 km (3 miles) to the northeast, Salona was the capital of Roman Dalmatia. It was a cultural centre with an arena, theatre, temples and baths, as well as a later addition of 30-odd churches. Plunder by the Avars and Slavs and some early local vandalism have reduced the site to mere foundations and fragments scattered over a hillside. However, look out for the 2nd-century amphitheatre and the remains of the 5th-century cathedral, with three aisles and a baptistry still visible. Just north of here is an interesting archaeological reserve area, incorporating the Tusculum museum, and excavations such as the Manastirine, a cemetery for Christian martyrs. On the way

you'll see the aqueduct that Diocletian had built to supply water to his palace. It still carries water to Split from the Jadro River.

Klis

Northeast from Salona is the massive Turkish fortress of Klis, scene of a heroic but unsuccessful siege by Croatian nationalists in 1537. A stroll along the high ramparts gives you a magnificent panorama of the surrounding countryside and the islands offshore.

VISIONS IN THE MOUNTAIN

Medjugorje was just an anonymous village, as unremarkable as any other to be found in the strange limestone mountains around Mostar in Bosnia-Herzegovina. Then, on June 24, 1981, six local teenagers saw an apparition of the Virgin Mary on one of the hilltops.

In the face of deep scepticism from the Yugoslav authorities and strict interrogation by the Catholic Church, the youths never faltered in their conviction that they had witnessed a true vision of the Madonna that day; indeed, the sightings continued. Before long, coach-parties bearing pilgrims from as far away as Ireland and the US began arriving to worship at the Church of St James, the local church, and to see the Hill of Apparitions. Just as quickly, new hotels sprang up, restaurants were built and souvenir sellers swept into town. Medjugorje was transformed into an Eastern European version of Lourdes. During the 1980s, 10 million people made the journey to this remote spot, although the Catholic Church has never officially accepted that a miracle occurred here.

The pilgrimages died down with the onset of the Bosnian War in the mid-1990s, but it is once again possible to visit Medjugorje from Split and Dubrovnik. There are church services every day, but the most important feasts celebrate the original apparition on June 24, the Assumption of the Virgin on August 15 and the Nativity of the Virgin on September 8.

SOUTHERN DALMATIAN COAST

Brač, Hvar, Vis, Korčula, Pelješac Peninsula,
Mljet, Dubrovnik, Lokrum, Cavtat

Whether you travel by boat or by road, the journey south from Split is awe-inspiring. The mainland is dominated by Dubrovnik, the undisputed "pearl of the Adriatic", which should be the ultimate centrepiece of any visit to the region. A jewelbox of a walled, medieval city, it is one of those rare places that always lives up to expectations. Out on the islands, meanwhile, southern Dalmatia can boast stylish Hvar, the sunniest spot in Croatia, and picture-book Korčula, a Venetian citadel jutting into the sea.

Brač

Brač has been coveted for its natural riches for two thousand years. It was here that the stone for Diocletian's palace was quarried, and a long procession of subsequent invaders have shown a marked taste for its bountiful crop of figs, grapes, olives and almonds. A 45-minute ferry ride from Split, the island is a delightful haven for beach-lovers, hikers and anyone wanting to ease the tensions of city life.

St Mary Magdalene's church in the pretty village of Svirce east of Hvar Town.

On the south side of the island, the medieval port of Bol has fine beaches nearby such as the famous Zlatni Rat, a striking sandy promontory jutting into the clear waters of the Adriatic. If it looks different from photographs you might have seen, don't be concerned—Zlatni Rat is constantly changing shape due to the effects of the wind. Bol is also well placed for hiking to old villages and the Vidova Mountain, the highest peak in the Adriatic islands.

Hvar

Hvar is often trumpeted as the loveliest Dalmatian island—that it is also the sunniest place in Croatia may have something to do with it. Indeed, the hotels promise a special discount in the winter months if there's snow or fog or the temperature drops below freezing. To add to Hvar's dreamy beauty, there's an abundance of wild flowers, with great fields of heather, rosemary and lavender, whose heady perfume pervades every corner of the island.

Hvar Town

Built around a pleasant harbour with a backdrop of steep hills and gardens that overflow with semi-tropical flowers, Hvar Town has retained its medieval charm. Pocket-sized Renaissance palaces, picturesque old monasteries and the blissful absence of cars combine with a yacht-studded harbour to create one of the Adriatic's most chic resorts.

Cathedral

The Renaissance St Stephen's Cathedral looks out on the main square (Trg Sveti Stjepana) east of the harbour. Its narrow trefoil façade is an elaborate trompe-l'œil, as it spans only the width of the nave, concealing the true size of the much larger church behind it. The main point of interest inside is a monumental 13th-century icon of the Virgin Mary.

Next door is the Bishop's Treasury, displaying chalices, reliquaries and embroidery.

Arsenal and Theatre

At the other end of the square, the huge Gothic Arsenal faces onto the harbour. It served mainly as a boathouse, and the great arch was wide enough to take in a Venetian warship for repairs.

Above the Arsenal, a real surprise awaits you. Intimately small and lavishly renovated at the beginning of the 19th century, the municipal theatre claims to be the earliest in Europe. It was constructed on top of the existing building in 1612. It's well worth finding out if anything is being staged while you are here, just so you can enjoy the experience.

Franciscan Monastery

If you head south along the harbour, you will come to a 15th-century Franciscan monastery, containing a good museum of Venetian paintings in the former refectory. The highlight of the collection is a superb *Last Supper* attributed to Matteo Ingoli.

Old Town

Opposite the Arsenal, to the right of the Renaissance loggia topped with Venetian lions, head up the steps to the walled old town. When the Turks raided Hvar in 1571, the townspeople fled this way to the Venetian fortress at the top of the hill. Overlooking the town and its harbour, the fortress offers panoramic views as well as a small museum of underwater archaeology.

Pakleni Otoci

If you need a refreshing dip in the sea after the climb up to the fortress, the best places for bathing are the sandy beaches of the beautiful Pakleni Otoci—Hell's Islands—just offshore.

Stari Grad

Some 20 km (12 miles) north of Hvar Town, Stari Grad was originally founded by the Ancient Greeks as a *pharos*, or lighthouse, from which the island's name derives. It was the capital of Hvar until the 14th century and today boasts many fine old streets and a scenic harbour. During your explorations, look for the 16th-century mansion of the renowned Croatian poet Petar Hektorović (1487–1572), with its attractive fish pond and garden.

Vis

One of the outermost Dalmatian islands, Vis is a peaceful place with a remarkable history. The Greeks founded the colony of Issa in the 4th century BC, bringing with them their wine-making skills. The island has been famous for its wines ever since. The Romans followed, to be succeeded by the Croatians, Byzantines, Venetians and Austrians. During the Napoleonic Wars, in 1811, the British defeated the French navy just off the coast and briefly occupied the island. And in World War II, Vis became Tito's headquarters and the base for the liberation of the mainland. The island is surrounded by a number of wrecks dating from Roman times to World War II, to the delight of divers.

Vis Town and Komiža are both delightful to visit. The latter is an attractive little fishing port, with a palm-lined crescent harbour,

SYMBOLIC FENCING

The *moreška*, a spectacular sabre dance that evokes Korčula's turbulent past and celebrates the victory of Good over Evil, is regularly performed by the men of the island between May and September. The combatants dress in splendid costumes of red and black, and confront each other in a thrilling clash of swords, with a beautiful bride as the prize. She symbolizes the lovely island of Korčula, of course, and the battle for her possession represents an age-old fight against invaders.

Venetian houses and mountain backdrop. It is a good base for trips to the Blue Cave on the isle of Biševo.

Korčula

Tradition has it that Korčula was founded by the Trojans in the 12th century BC, but in fact it was their old enemies, the Greeks, who colonized the island, calling it Korkyra Melaina (Black Korčula) because of its dark forests. All around the island, sandy bays and rocky inlets with crystal-clear water provide ideal spots for swimming. Korčula is a famous wine-producing island, and while you're here be sure to try some Grk, one of Croatia's best wines.

Korčula Town

Situated on a headland at the eastern end of the island, this small town is a tight cluster of narrow streets designed with an intriguing herringbone pattern: the streets facing west are straight, and those facing east are curved, a cunning medieval form of air-conditioning aimed at catching as much of the breeze as possible. The buildings are made from a honey-coloured stone that dazzles at noon and changes to a rich golden hue with the sunset. Korčulans claim that the famous traveller Marco Polo was born here.

Land Gate

Kopnena vrata, the entrance to the old town, was begun in 1391 and completed in 1495 with the addition of the square Revelin Tower. The north side of the gate is the superb Foscolo triumphal arch, built by Korčula's noblemen in 1650 to celebrate the Venetian governor's victory over the Turks. The grand town hall just in front of the gate perfectly illustrates the city's eminence under Venetian rule.

St Mark's Cathedral

The town's architectural masterpiece stands in all its flamboyant splendour on tiny Cathedral Square, straight ahead. Construction began in the early 15th cen-

ISLAND OF STONE

Although it's just a small dot in the Adriatic off the Korčula coast, the islet of Vrnik has had an impact on European architecture way beyond its size. Vrnik is famous for the quality and resilience of its clean white stone. In operation since Roman times, the islet's quarries have supplied the material for Korčula Town and the Rector's Palace in Dubrovnik, as well as such distant buildings as St Sofia's in Istanbul, the parliament in Vienna and even Stockholm's town hall.

tury and took 150 years to complete, incorporating on the way a change in styles from Gothic to Renaissance. Its finely carved portal, rose window and remarkable gables are testament to the skills of Korčula's masons, famous throughout Europe at the time. The highly ornamented belltower is capped by an octagonal lantern. In the interior you will find a Gothic baptistry, complete with 13th-century baptismal fonts. There are also some fine art works, including an altarpiece painting by Tintoretto of St Mark flanked by saints Jerome and Bartholomew.

Next door to the cathedral, the 14th-century Abbot's Palace

Korčulans claim that their town was the childhood home of Marco Polo.

houses an exquisite display of art and antiquities, with a collection that varies from ancient church robes to contemporary Croatian paintings.

Town Museum
Across the square, the 16th-century Gabrielis Palace houses a museum dedicated to local history and culture, in particular the traditional Korčula industries such as shipbuilding and stonemasonry.

Marco Polo's House
One block north of the cathedral and just round the corner past St Peter's Church (begun in the 10th century) is a tall building signposted as Marco Polo's birthplace. There's not a shred of evidence beyond local legend to support the claim, but it's still worth going inside for the view of Korčula from the tower. Afterwards, continue down the street to the ramparts.

City Walls
Until the mid-19th century, the town was completely encircled by a wall, built originally to defend it from Turkish invaders and marauding pirates. The remaining parts date mainly from the 14th-16th centuries, with the towers in especially good condition. 69

Icon Gallery and All Saints

Following the ramparts back towards the Land Gate, you'll reach the Icon Gallery in the southeast corner of the old town, in the rooms of the All Saints Brotherhood. There are several interesting Cretan icons here, and a 4th-century Madonna. The ticket also allows access to the Renaissance All Saints' Church (Svi Sveti), joined to the gallery by a covered bridge. Inside are several works of art and a fine baroque altarpiece comprising an 18th-century Pietà carved from walnut by George Raphael Donner.

Pelješac Peninsula

This narrow, 65-km (40-mile) peninsula seems barely attached to the mainland and stretches out into the Adriatic much like one of the nearby islands. It has several quiet and attractive resorts and two towns of particular interest.

Orebić

Just across the water from Korčula, Orebić is the main access point for travellers to the island. The town has some notable features that make it worth pausing awhile, however, especially for the enthusiastic hiker. It's impossible to miss stark, grey Sveti Ilija, the mountain just behind the town. There's a good trail that leads right to the top; it is signposted and can be picked up near the cathedral. The views on high are fantastic. Another trail leads up to a Franciscan monastery dating from 1470.

Back down at sea level, Orebić is blessed with several sandy beaches, which connoisseurs generally rate as better than those on Korčula.

Ston

At the entrance to the peninsula, its fortifications built into the steep cliffside, the salt-producing town of Ston is split into two different settlements, Veliki and Mali (Great and Small). Most of the houses were constructed in the 15th and 16th centuries, and there's a powerful fortress on top of the hill. The Republic of Dubrovnik, being keener on business than war, had bought the peninsula from its two claimants, the Bosnians and the Serbian king, in the 14th century for its agricultural richness. Ston was planned and built on the narrowest point on the isthmus purely in order to protect Dubrovnik's investment. It was damaged by earthquake in 1996 and many of its houses are still uninhabited.

Mljet

Located between Korčula and Dubrovnik, this is a popular island for day-trippers from both places. But Mljet more than merits a longer stay. Indeed, legend has it that Odysseus spent seven years here on his way back from the Trojan Wars, captivated by the nymph Calypso.

But even if you can only spare one night, it will at least allow you the chance to put up at the 12th-century Benedictine monastery situated in the middle of Veliko Jezero, a picturesque salt lake in the Mljet National Park on the western part of the island. Converted into a comfortable hotel, the monastery sits on a delightful islet covered in Mljet's famous Aleppo pines and boasting good beaches for bathing. The lakeshore provides an excellent spot for walking and enjoying the island's natural beauty.

One thing you won't have to worry about bumping into on Mljet is a snake. At the turn of the century, the authorities introduced the mongoose, the snake's deadly enemy, to the island. Today there are no snakes but an awful lot of mongooses.

Dubrovnik

In the Middle Ages, Dubrovnik's sophisticated diplomacy made it an independent city-state rivalling Venice in the extent of its maritime trade. Indeed, such was the size and fame of its fleet that the word "argosy", deriving from the city's former name of Ragusa, became a synonym for a merchant treasure-ship. However, the city was devastated by earthquake in 1667 and never recovered its former glory. Centuries of independence finally came to an end in 1806, when Napoleon conquered the whole region. Dubrovnik passed to the Austrians nine years later.

If the locals thought Dubrovnik had settled into a life of peaceful Mediterranean-style tourism they were wrong. Disaster struck in 1991, when the town came under intense shellfire from the Yugoslav National Army, causing unprecedented damage to rooftops and buildings. But Dubrovnik has demonstrated a Phoenix-like capacity for rising from the ashes —thanks to UNESCO and several international trusts. There are still pockmarks on some of the old houses, but the city is a glorious place to follow your whim and simply wander around, be it on top of the imposing city walls, along the Placa, the immaculate main drag, or through the maze of picturesquely steep side-streets, with their outdoor markets and all but hidden gardens, churches and mansions.

Pile Gate

Entering the medieval old town from new Dubrovnik is like travelling back into the city's golden Renaissance past. For the ancient paved stone streets, churches and palaces have retained their age-

less beauty, and such modern bugbears as the motor car are banned. This unique adventure in time-travel usually begins by crossing a wooden drawbridge and going through the Gothic arch of the Pile Gate. Notice the statue of St Blaise above the arch, one of a number of representations of Dubrovnik's patron saint, who is venerated for having helped repel a Venetian attack a thousand years ago.

City Walls

The best place to get an overview of the whole rich pageant is from on top of Dubrovnik's pride and joy, the magnificent city walls, reached from just inside the Pile Gate. Nearly 2 km (over a mile) in circumference, the fortifications date mainly from the 15th and 16th centuries and include fifteen towers, five bastions, two corner towers and a fortress. In some places the walls are up to 6 m (almost 20 ft) thick—enough to have withstood both the earthquake of 1667 and the bombardment of 1991. The best panorama is from the highest tower, Minčeta, at the northwest corner of the wall. This great round fortress, begun in the 14th century and worked on by such great architects as Michelozzo Michelozzi and Juraj Dalmatinac, symbolizes the power of the ancient city-state.

One of the most exhilarating walks anywhere in the world is to go on a complete circuit of the ramparts. It will take you about an hour, during which time you will be rewarded by unforgettable perspectives over the terracotta roofs of the city, the bougainvillaea-splashed gardens and the sparkling waters of the Adriatic.

Onofrio's Great Fountain

Descending from the walls at Pile Gate, you are confronted by a massive 15th-century fountain, named after its Neapolitan architect, Onofrio della Cava. He specialized in waterworks, and this handsome, 16-sided reservoir is the biggest of his many fountains. The water was supplied by a system he designed using an 11-km (6.5-mile) aqueduct starting high in the mountains.

Our Saviour's Church

Facing the fountain, the tiny church (Sveti Spas) has a Renaissance façade and a Gothic interior. Remarkably, it escaped destruction in the 1667 earthquake that damaged much of the city. The church is now used for art exhibitions.

Franciscan Monastery

Behind Sveti Spas, and overshadowing it, the imposing church of the Franciscan monastery is entered through a richly decorated 73 main portal. The monastery complex was originally built in the early 14th century and acted as a defensive watchtower for the Pile Gate as well as a house of worship.

In its delightful gardened cloister lined with slender octagonal columns, a chemist's shop dating from 1317—one of the oldest in Europe—has been restored down to the last apothecary jar, mortar and pestle.

Placa

The Placa (pronounced *platsa*), also called the Stradun, is old Dubrovnik's great, straight principal thoroughfare paved with large flat slippery slabs of stone. The architecture on either side is a model of harmony, where the houses—all of them four storeys tall with arched doorways—are of the same light-coloured stone as the street itself. Their unpretentious baroque façades are an afterthought, added after the devastation of the 17th-century earthquake.

The Placa is still the ancient city's most animated artery. During the day, it's alive with the bustle of shops, pavement cafés and restaurants, while around sunset the street fills with families enjoying their traditional *korzo*, the leisurely Mediterranean-style evening promenade.

Jewish Museum

Located in the narrow Žudioska Street off Placa to the left, the museum is housed in Europe's second-oldest synagogue (the oldest is in Prague). It contains a small but valuable collection of sacred Jewish art and important documents relating to the history of Dubrovnik's Jewish community.

THE FIVE BEST FESTIVALS In the summer all of Croatia breaks out in cultural excitement. Along the coast, Pula's Roman amphitheatre becomes a cinema for the **Croatian International Film Festival**; the **Dubrovnik Summer Festival** takes over the city's ancient palaces and churches with music, ballet, drama and art; and the **Zagreb Summer Festival** puts on open-air concerts and plays. At Koprivnica, near the Hungarian border, an unusual **Naïve Art Festival** is held in June, while Eastern Slavonia's Đakovo is the venue for July's **Festival of National Costumes**.

Luža

The square at the east end of the Placa is surrounded by restaurants, cafés, a cinema and several of Dubrovnik's finest buildings.

Reconstructed in 1929, the municipal clock tower has been tolling the hours since the 15th century. Striking the bell, bronze clappers shaped like soldiers are symbols of Dubrovnik, known as the "green men".

Nearby is a delightful Renaissance fountain popularly referred to as Onofrio's Small Fountain, although it's now known to be the work of another Italian master, Pietro Martini.

In the centre of the square, Orlando's Column dates from 1419. Proclamations used to be read from the top by the town crier, while the base was the place for punishing criminals.

Sponza Palace

Built by local craftsmen between 1517 and 1523, the palace on the Luža is an elegant example of mixed Gothic-Renaissance architecture. This was the republic's all-important customs house and mint, and now contains the state archives.

Dominican Monastery

Behind the palace, the huge Dominican monastery once protected the city's eastern gate. The church museum contains an interesting collection of silver reliquaries and chalices, and sumptuous jewellery given as votive gifts by the Dubrovnik nobility. There are some fine religious paintings from the 15th and 16th centuries, especially those by the Croatian Nikola Božidarević, and a work by Titian, a picture of St Blaise with St Magdalene.

Church of St Blaise

Back on the Luža, the Church of St Blaise (Sveti Vlaho) stands on a balustraded platform just south of Orlando's Column, and is the sumptuous Italian baroque successor to a much damaged 14th-century church. Look out for the silver statue of St Blaise behind the altar holding a model of the walled city. It is as accurate as a modern map, and provides a detailed record as to what the city looked like before the earthquake in 1667.

Rector's Palace

Across from St Blaise's, the Gothic Rector's Palace (Knežev Dvor), Dubrovnik's most impressive building, is a 15th-century restoration by Michelozzo Michelozzi after the medieval building was largely destroyed by an accidental gunpowder explosion. Here the city-state's supreme leader, elected for only a one-month term of office, received petitioners and foreign diplomats. 75

The palace's grand staircase, leading down from an arcaded balcony to the perfectly proportioned courtyard inside the entrance, is particularly elegant. The building now houses a museum exhibiting 17th-century paintings, period furniture, coins and weaponry.

Cathedral

On the south side of the square, the baroque cathedral replaced a 12th-century church destroyed in the 1667 earthquake. It contains some interesting artworks, including a large polyptych of the Assumption by Titian. The treasury features a 12th-century Byzantine crown said to contain a relic of St Blaise himself.

Jesuit Church

If you walk west from the cathedral and turn left at Gundalić Square, you will immediately see the *Skalinada*, a superb staircase of 1735 modelled on the Spanish Steps in Rome. These lead up to Dubrovnik's third major post-earthquake baroque edifice, the Jesuit Church, completed in the 1720s and the city's largest.

Harbour

A gate in the city wall between the cathedral and the Rector's Palace leads to the old harbour, where warships and treasure ships used to bob at anchor in the republic's heyday. In the 16th century it became so crowded that the principal port was moved further west to Gruž.

From the old harbour, take a ferry across to Lokrum Island, 10 minutes away, for an afternoon swim, or else just sit in the shade at the outdoor café and enjoy the little port's pleasing hubbub.

Near the southern hook of the old harbour, there's an aquarium in St John's Fortress and above it a maritime museum that concentrates on Dubrovnik's 16th-century Golden Age.

Lokrum

A stone's throw from Dubrovnik, this tiny island packs in a lot of history. Lokrum is the place, it is said, where Richard the Lion-Heart was shipwrecked on his return from the Third Crusade in 1192. In gratitude for his rescue, he contributed funds towards Dubrovnik's original cathedral.

The Benedictine monastery, located just back from where the ferry docks, was founded in the 11th century. The monks brought many exotic flora with them, a tradition that continues at the nearby Botanical Garden in the centre of the island, where plants and trees from Australia and South America are testament to the region's sultry climate.

Lokrum also has a French-built star-shaped fortress from the time of Napoleon's Illyrian Provinces,

Seen from on high, the old town of Dubrovnik looks like a scale model.

enjoying great views across to Dubrovnik, and a mansion constructed in 1859 for the Habsburg Archduke Maximilian. He was crowned Emperor of Mexico in 1864, only to face rebellion and execution three years later.

For an island so close to the city, Lokrum has a suprisingly back-to-nature atmosphere. There are pinewoods for shady walks and several rocky beaches, including a well-known FKK (nudist) beach.

Cavtat

After the resort town of Cavtat, 15 km (9 miles) southeast of Dubrovnik, Croatia tapers away to the border with Montenegro. Cavtat was the ancient Greek town of Epidaurum, whose inhabitants fled from barbarian invasions in the 7th century and founded a new city on a site easier to defend—Dubrovnik. The town is in a very picturesque setting, planted in a forest of pine and cypress on a peninsula called Rat. It has ancient streets, Gothic and Renaissance churches and palaces to explore, sand dunes and some fine beaches to lounge on as well.

On a hill overlooking the town is the great, incongruous Račić Mausoleum, the work of Ivan Meštrović.

Cultural Notes

Croatian Literature

The 16th-century playwright Marin Držić, known for his comedies, is touted as the Croatian Shakespeare, a forerunner to Molière in European drama. Ivan Gundulić (1588–1638), influenced by Italian poetry, represents the Republic of Dubrovnik's literary highwater mark in the 17th century. Later writers worth seeking out include Miroslav Krleža (1893–1981), whose works such as *The Return of Philip Latinovicz* sparked a revival in Croatian literature in the 1930s; Pavao Pavlicic, writer of detective novels set in Zagreb; and his contemporary Dubravka Ugrešić, a woman novelist whose work acutely dissects modern Croatian society since independence. For a more popular, journalistic perspective on recent history, read Slavenka Drakulić's book *Balkan Express: Fragments from the Other Side of War*.

Juraj Dalmatinac

Ever since Diocletian's magnificent palace was constructed at the end of the 3rd century, the Dalmatian coast has been known for the skill of its builders and the beauty of its locally quarried stone. This combination reached its pinnacle with the great Renaissance architect and sculptor, Juraj Dalmatinac (George of Dalmatia). He was born in Zadar around 1410, but little is known about his life. It is certain that he studied in Italy in the 1430s, absorbing the new ideas of Brunelleschi and Donatello, and that he returned to Croatia by the end of the decade. His work is a brilliant development of the transitional, or mixed Gothic-Renaissance style, and can be seen in Dubrovnik, Split and Pag. But his enduring memorial is the remarkable Šibenik Cathedral. Dalmatinac died in 1473 and never saw his masterpiece completed: it wasn't finished until the 16th century, when Dalmatinac's plans were finally realised as a perfect vision in stone.

Korzo

Citizens of the Adriatic towns are proud to be Croatian, but they also share a cultural heritage with their Mediterranean neighbours. This is never more clear than at the end of each day, when the sun sets and the air cools to a pleasant temperature. It's then that people fill the streets and enjoy the famous *korzo*—an early-evening stroll taken en masse. Split's *korzo* has the reputation as Croatia's most stylish, whereas Dubrovnik's inhabitants have the advantage of parading along the elegant Placa. But whatever the town, the point, of course, is to see and be seen.

This is people-watching taken to the level of art, and participants are as uninhibited about studying each other as they would be gazing at a painting on a wall. Best of all, it's a Croatian tradition that anyone can join in. When the last glow of the sun touches Dalmatia's rooftops, you'll find it's perfectly natural to get out onto the streets and stroll along like a local.

Ivan Meštrović

Born in 1883, Croatia's paramount modern artist began his working life as a shepherd boy in the Dalmatian mountains. His natural talent for carving soon became apparent, and he was apprenticed to a marble cutter at the age of 13. Within three years he was at the Vienna Academy, and he became part of the Secession movement at the turn of the century. Never one to be bogged down in theories of art, he moved on to live and work in Paris and exhibited around Europe, becoming in 1915 the first living artist to have a one-man show at the Victoria and Albert Museum in London. Constantly inspired by his love of Michelangelo, Meštrović was acclaimed by such luminaries as Rodin—who called him the "biggest phenomenon among sculptors". His works are monumental, figurative, visionary and innately religious. Characterized by classical, bold cutting, they can be seen around the world, from Zagreb and Split to the famous monument dedicated to the American Indians in Chicago. He is buried at the huge Meštrović family tomb, which he designed in 1930 in his childhood village of Otavice.

Naïve Art

The most significant development in Croatian art since World War II has been the amazing success of its naïve artists. Known as the Hlebine School, after the town northeast of Zagreb where the most prominent artists come from, they are untrained peasant-painters whose freedom from conventional perspective and realistic tone creates canvases of extraordinary colour and intensity. Subjects include anything that touches the painter's rural life—the countryside as it changes through the seasons, farm animals, Christianity—coupled with occasionally anomalies from popular culture, where for no logical reason the Eiffel Tower or even Sophia Loren might appear in the setting of an ordinary Croatian village.

In the hands of its best exponents, such as Ivan Generalić, Ivan Lacković Croata and Ivan Rabuzin, the naïve style can be surprising, amusing and deeply moving. The two most important centres for viewing this art are Hlebine, where there's a Gallery of Naïve Art and the Museum Collection of Ivan Generalić, and Zagreb, whose Museum of Naïve Art has more than a thousand works.

79

$Shopping$

Fashionable boutiques and department stores can be found in Zagreb around Ilica, the main shopping street, while up-market shops in Dubrovnik and Split sell stylish clothes and leatherware. But old crafts have survived. In little markets or even on roadside stalls, look out for delicate lacework, hand-painted pottery and locally made cheeses and honey.

Art

For a souvenir with a difference, consider a painting or drawing. The naïve school produces often appealing, sometimes startling images of rural Croatia.

Croatiana

Two things which the Croatians are proud to have thought of first are the ballpoint pen and the cravat. Souvenir replicas of Slavoljub Penkala's pen, patented in 1906 and thus beating Mr Biro by more than 30 years, and the cravat from Hrvatska, complete with leaflet explaining its origins, make amusing mementos.

Gifts from the various regions might include lavender oil from Hvar, a *bokaleta*, or wine goblet, from Istria, or the Slavonian *samica*, a musical instrument made of aromatic wood. More common souvenirs, which you will find all over the country, include brightly painted pottery, dolls in national costume—and the full-size costumes themselves—and items of carved wood.

Croatian folk music, with specific regional styles, can be bought on tape or compact disc at any record shop; it ranges from haunting vocal arrangements to spirited instrumental pieces.

Food and Drink

Delicious ewe's-milk cheese from Pag, *kulen* sausage and *pršut* ham, salted olives grown on the islands, or honey from the Krajina region will retain the special flavour of Croatia after you have returned home. If you find a Croatian wine you enjoy it might be an idea to invest in a few bottles, as very little of it is exported. *Šljivovica* plum brandy is as emblematic of the country as the *šahovnica*, Croatia's red-and-white chequerboard flag, and it is sure to bring back warm memories with each sip.

Handicrafts

True to its background as frontier to Ottoman lands, Croatia is an excellent place for obtaining carpets. Hand-loomed, and bearing striking and original patterns, they are certainly worth looking out for.

The pace of life is slower on the islands, and traditional skills have managed to survive the onslaught of mass production. The Dalmatian islands of Pag, Hvar and Lepoglava in particular are noted for the quality of their embroidery, which can embellish anything from handkerchiefs to blouses and dresses, and for lace made from agave fibres. Elsewhere, woven tablecloths, shoulder bags and dress materials decorated with typical Croatian patterns always make distinctive gifts. Croatia is also known for its first-rate craftsmen working in crystal, porcelain, ceramics and copperware.

Leather Goods

Footwear and leather goods often have the artisanal touch. Bargains are still there to be had, and you will find attractive shoes, bags, wallets and luggage at the markets that enliven most Croatian towns, although you will want to check the price and quality before making a purchase.

Say "cheese": something to try with the local wine.

Dining Out

Thanks to its special knack of adopting the best of what the many conquerors and traders who came this way had to offer, Croatia's cuisine is an exciting blend of foreign influences tempered by local tastes. The Venetians brought pasta, the Austrians cakes and the Hungarians goulash. Croatia's historic proximity to the Turkish empire is responsible for ultra-sweet desserts and strong black coffee. The profusion of fresh fish is due entirely to the generosity of the Adriatic Sea.

Breakfast

The Croatians do not breakfast like kings, as the old saying recommends, but prefer to fortify themselves with a strong coffee (*kava*) and perhaps a *burek*, a large, round pastry filled with cheese (*sir*) or meat (*meso*), and seen on the counters of bakeries, food shops and corner stores alike throughout the country. Most hotels provide a buffet breakfast with cereals, yoghourt, ham, cheese and eggs.

Appetizers

Some might argue that the hors d'œuvres are the best part of the meal in Croatia, and you could fill yourself up with mouth-watering ease long before the main course is in sight. Wind-dried Dalmatian smoked ham (*istarski* or *Dalmatinski pršut*) is justly famous for its subtle flavour and texture, and the local salami (*gavrilovićeva salama*) is excellent. *Kajmak* (pronounced kay-muck), squares made from the skin of scalded milk and cream, is something new to discover.

Especially popular around the Zagreb region, *štrukli* is an all-purpose dish whose basic format of cottage cheese in a thin dough can be either baked or boiled with any number of sweet or savoury fillings. Cheese is regarded as a starter in Croatia—try *Paški sir*, a hard, strong cheese from the island of Pag. *Trapist* cheese was originally made by monks, and now comes in regional variations.

Main Courses

Sooner or later your nose will lead you to the sizzle of meat grilling on charcoal (*roštilj*).

Tucking into dinner in a friendly Zagreb restaurant.

Items range from small, sausage-shaped rolls of beef or beef and pork *(ćevapčići)*, to large hamburger steaks *(pljeskavica)* or skewered pieces of pork or veal *(ražnjići)*. All this and more can be combined in a huge mixed grill *(mješano meso)*.

Djuveč is a goulash of lamb or pork with rice, green peppers, aubergine and other vegetables. *Sarma* are meat-stuffed cabbage leaves. A meat, rice and tomato stuffing also goes into green peppers to make *punjene paprike*.

A dish you are likely to encounter in the interior is *manistra od bobića* (beans and corn soup), which is sure to fill you up.

Slavonia, in the east of the country, boasts the prized spicy *kulen* sausage, while around Zagreb *mlinci*, a sheet of pasta, baked till crispy then broken into pieces and soaked in hot water, accompanies turkey and duck.

Unsurprisingly, perhaps, for an area so long under the cultural sway of Italy, the Dalmatian coast is a good place for pasta and pizza. On the Istrian peninsula, influenced by Italian and Austrian cuisine, you may find yourself one day eating pasta with truffles (fungi for which Istria is famous) and the next tucking into Istrian *jota*, a flavourful stew with sauerkraut and ham.

Fish and Seafood

With over 350 different species of fish in the Adriatic, it will come as no surprise that there's a wide range of fish dishes to be found in Croatian cooking. Most common are mackerel and sardines. Bass, dentex or bream grilled over coals or poached (*lešo*) are delicious. *Brodet* is a strongly flavoured fish stew, often served with *palenta*, a cake of ground maize (cornmeal). Steamed mussels tossed in rice are another speciality.

Lobster (*jastog*) and crab—usually served cold with mayonnaise—are delicious but expensive. Oyster fans should seek out those cultivated in Ston Bay near the Peljesac peninsula, just north of Dubrovnik, and known internationally for their quality. Squid, sea-dates, cuttlefish and octopus are found all along the coast, and there will be almost as many different ways of cooking them as there are Adriatic islands. Octopus, for example, is traditionally eaten dried with eggs on Rab, boiled on Pag and roasted in white wine on Hvar.

Vegetarian Dishes

Croatia is a resolutely meat- and fish-eating culture, but there are some glimmers of hope for the vegetarian traveller. Look out for such tasty delights as aubergine steamed in olive oil (*tikvice va*

lešo), various stews such as green bean and pumpkin, or *grah salata*, onion and bean salad.

Desserts

Turkish and Viennese influences account for the very rich desserts, embellished with nuts, poppy seeds and cream. Richest of all is *baklava*, an imported Turkish creation of flaky filo pastry interleaved with nuts and drenched in a lemony honey syrup. *Orahnjača* is another lip-smacking walnut confection. A variety of strudels, including plum, apple and sour cherry, reflect northern Croatia's past role as the Austrian Empire's greatest resort area. Pancakes (*palačinke*) can be stuffed with jam, ground walnuts, chocolate or cream cheese.

Drinks

Wine-making really got underway in Croatia after the Romans conquered the country in the 2nd century BC. Today, there are vineyards producing decent-quality red (*crno*, "black" —a good indication of the full-bodied nature of Croatian wine) and white (*bjelo*) wines all around the country.

Sampling a wine from the region in which you find yourself can be a rewarding experience. On the Istrian peninsula try Merlot, a fruity, deep-red wine, or Teran, another rich-tasting red. In northern Croatia look out for Kut-

Local herbs are gathered to flavour home-made spirits, sold on the markets in unlabelled bottles.

jevo and Traminac. Croatia's best wines come from the Dalmatian coast. Hvar produces Zlatan Plavac, made from a full, spicy red grape, as well as Yaretna, a fine, dry white. Further south, Grk, from the island of Korčula, is a flavoursome white that's as crisp as its name. Dingač, local to the Pelješac peninsula, is another strong red that's perfect for accompanying one of Croatia's meaty dishes. The locals often temper an ordinary house red with still water *(bevanda)* and white with carbonated *(gemišt)*, especially at lunchtime.

If you're in need of something stronger, try one of the fiery fruit alcohols *(rakija)* such as the famous *šljivovica* plum brandy or *lozovača,* a grape brandy. Restaurants often offer a complimentary glass at the end of the meal so that you can leave with a warm glow. The local fire-water in Dalmatia is *travarica*, a strong brandy tempered by juniper and myrtle herbs.

Croatian lager *(pivo)* is excellent. The most popular kinds are Karlovačko, made in Karlovac, and Ožujsko, from the Zagreb area. Imported brands from the rest of Europe and the US are available, and Guinness seems to be catching on, but these always cost more than the local beer.

85

Sports

Croatians are big sports fans, and if they aren't transfixed by a game of football (soccer) or basketball on TV, they might well be engaged in some sporting activity themselves. It's understandable that watersports head the list, but there are other ways to burn off excess energy, playing tennis, for example, or heading inland to the mountains and national parks.

Water Sports

With calm, warm and exceptionally clean water along its coast, Croatia is a haven for any number of sea-based sports. The swimming is good in most places, although it probably pays to be wary of beaches close to the industrial ports of Rijeka, Pula and Split. The clear waters and interesting marine life of the coast also make it an excellent place for snorkelling and scuba diving—an activity that's becoming increasingly popular. Windsurfing can be enjoyed all along the seafront, early summer being the time to pick up the best winds. You can also try your hand at water-skiing or paragliding.

Boating

Croatia's Adriatic coast is a magnet for yachtsmen from around the world. Even if you don't actually own a yacht, you can always hire one (with a group of people the costs can be reasonable) or a smaller sailing boat. The reward is the chance to sail around stunning, unspoilt islands, dropping anchor at uninhabited coves of pristine beauty. For those who want a more physical engagement with the sea, sea-kayaking provides an unforgettable way to see the Croatian coast.

Fishing

Croatia offers good opportunities for both sea- and fresh-water fishing, although before you cast your line be sure to find out what the rules are for the stretch of water you plan to fish in. You will also need to buy a permit. Check where these can be obtained at the local port authority or tourist office.

Hiking and Climbing

Croatia's national parks provide some superb hiking areas. Try the Risnjak National Park east of Rijeka, snow-covered in winter. Or the Paklenica National Park, near Zadar on the southern slopes of Mt Velebit, with dramatic canyons and forest scenery.

Among the popular mountain-climbing locations are the Gorski Kotar region not far from the Slovenian border in the north, Mt Učka, with a peak at 1,396 m (4,579 ft), near Rijeka, and all along the Dinaric Alps.

Riding

Horses and mountain-bikes can be hired for cross-country treks, particularly around the Istrian peninsula, the Kvarner Gulf region or Vrana lake, also famous for fishing and birdwatching.

Hunting

Hunting isn't especially frowned upon in Croatia, and you can pursue wild boar, deer, partridge and other wild fowl, and even bears. The larger animals are hunted most notably around the mountainous Gorski Kotar area.

Skiing

The main ski resorts are Sljeme on Mt Medvednica, which has cross-country and downhill, and Bjelolašica in the Gorski Katar range, boasting seven ski runs.

Scaling a rock face in Paklenica National Park.

Airports

There are nine airports in Croatia: Zagreb, Split, Dubrovnik, Pula, Zadar, Rijeka, Osijek, Lošinj and Brač. Croatia Airlines has regular flights to Zagreb from several European and North American cities. Most of these continue on to Split and Dubrovnik. Other international carriers such as BA, Lufthansa and Air France also fly to Zagreb.

Zagreb's Pleso Airport lies 17 km (10 miles) southeast of the capital. The Eurokont airport bus leaves once an hour for the centre, and there are also taxis. The terminal has currency exchange, car-hire and tourist information facilities, as well as duty-free shop, café and bar services. During the summer season charter planes provide a direct service from abroad to airports in popular tourist destinations such as Split, Dubrovnik and Pula.

Climate

Croatia has two distinct climates, one coastal and the other typical of southeast Europe's continental interior.

The Adriatic coast has a Mediterranean climate with an annual average of 2,600 hours of sunshine. Summers are hot, dry and mostly sunny. Spring and early summer are warm, but cooled by the *maestral* winds, while autumn temperatures are pleasant, with warm seas. Winters are generally mild and wet, although Istria and northern Dalmatia receive unwelcome visits by a chilly northeast wind known as the *bura*.

The mountainous Croatian interior, without the warming influence of the Mediterranean to protect it from cold northern winds, has a significantly harsher winter, with average January temperatures of between –2° and 2°C (28° and 36°F) and frequent snowfall. Summers are usually warm and dry.

Communications

Post Offices. Open Monday to Friday 7 a.m.–8 p.m., Saturday 7 a.m.–2 p.m. In tourist resorts in high season, they may be open until 10 p.m. as well as on Sundays. The post office at Zagreb's Central Bus Station provides services 24 hours a day. Post offices also have telephone and fax facilities.

Telephone. The country code for Croatia is 385. The area code for Split is 21, Zagreb 1, and Dubrovnik 20. To call Split from abroad, for example, dial your appropriate international access code + 385 + 21 + local number.

The access code for international calls out of Croatia is 00.

Public phones in Croatia can only be used with a phonecard. These can be purchased at post offices, newspaper kiosks and tobacconists (although in smaller towns you may find that only post offices sell them).

Larger hotels offer Internet facilities, and there are plenty of Internet cafés in towns and cities around the country.

Consulates

Embassies and consulates are in Zagreb, although the UK also maintains consulates in Split and Dubrovnik. These should only be contacted in case of serious emergencies, lost passports or worse, and *not* for lost tickets or money.

Driving

If you drive to Croatia, you will need an insurance green card to enter. Alternatively, you may wish to hire a car once you are there. Car rental offices are located at airports, towns and cities and in the larger resorts. All the main international companies are represented plus local firms at competitive prices. The big firms offer the possibility of one-way rental at no extra cost, however. When hiring a car you will need a valid driving licence. Some com-

panies have a minimum age limit of 18 while others stipulate 21, so always telephone to make sure first if it might be a problem.

Although public transport services are efficient and extensive, hiring a car allows ready access to some of the country's most beautiful areas. There are good-quality motorways around Zagreb, while brand new motorways now link the capital to Rijeka and the Istrian peninsula and to the Dalmatian coast. These are all toll roads. Be warned that the beautiful coast road (the Jadranska Magistrala) and the spectacular route through the Dinaric Alps—are hair-raisingly mountainous and often frustratingly slow in summer. Overtaking sometimes seems to be more a question of luck than judgement, so it might be better to sit back, enjoy the scenery and arrive at your destination a little later than planned. The speed limits on Croatia's roads are 130 kph on dual-carriage motorways, 90 kph on highways, and 60 kph in residential areas unless otherwise signposted. The maximum speed for cars with trailers is 80 kph. It is illegal to overtake a long line of slow-moving cars or trucks (except on a dual carriageway).

Road information is available from the Croatian Automobile Club (*Hrvatski Auto-klub* or HAK), tel. (01) 4640-800, round the clock. HAK road assistance can be obtained nationwide, tel. 987.

Fuel prices are comparable with those in most Western European countries. Although larger petrol stations accept credit cards, it's a good idea to have enough cash on hand if you find yourself at a small town or village pump.

Electric Current
The standard is 220-volt, 50-cycle A.C. Sockets take the standard European twin round prongs. British and American electronic equipment will require an adaptor and possibly a transformer.

Emergencies
Emergency telephone numbers:
Police   92
Fire brigade 93
Ambulance   94

Formalities
Holders of EU, American, Canadian, Australian and New Zealand passports do not require visas to enter Croatia. Other visitors should check with the nearest Croatian Embassy before departure. All foreign visitors must register with the police when they arrive, although your hotel will probably do this for you automatically after you have checked in.

The following goods may be imported by each passenger: 200 cigarettes or 50 cigars or 250 g tobacco; 1 litre wine and 1 litre spirits; 1/4 litre eau de cologne and 1 bottle of perfumes.

For non-residents there is no limit on the import or export of foreign currencies, and you can take in or out of the country up to the value of HRK 15,000 in local currency.

When leaving the country, be aware that if you have bought any religious artefacts or art works, you may need an export permit from the government's department of Cultural and Natural Heritage. Always check when you make your purchase.

Health
The biggest risk to health is spending too much time in the strong Mediterranean sunshine. It is best to avoid excessive exposure to it, especially during the middle of the day, and it is always a good idea to wear a hat and use a sun-block cream. Drink plenty of mineral water to avoid dehydration. You will need to take a supply of mosquito repellent.

Visitors from countries with reciprocal health agreements with Croatia will receive free medical treatment at hospitals *(bolnica)* or medical centres *(dom zdravlja)*. There are standard charges that must be paid, although these are relatively low. If you are from a country without a reciprocal agreement, it is worth investing in travel insurance before you leave home.

Holidays

January 1	New Year
January 6	Epiphany
May 1	Labour Day
June 22	Croatian National Uprising Day
June 25	Statehood Day
August 5	Thanksgiving Day
August 15	Assumption
October 8	Independence Day
November 1	All Saints' Day
December 25	Christmas
December 26	St Stephen's Day

Moveable: Good Friday, Easter Monday, Corpus Christi

Language

Croatian is a Slavic language written in the Latin alphabet. For speakers of other European languages, pronunciation of written Croatian is fairly straightforward, but there are a few Slavic idiosyncracies: *š* is pronounced "sh"; *ž* sounds like the "s" in "measure"; *ć* and *č* both give a "ch" sound. A *j* is pronounced like the "y" in "yellow", while *dz* is pronounced like the "j" in "just".

You will probably find that you don't need to struggle too long over finding the right Croatian word. With centuries of foreign rule and a longstanding cosmopolitan interest in other languages and cultures, Croatians often speak at least one other language. Due to the traditional influence of Austria and Germany in the region, German is widely spoken. Italian is understood on the Adriatic coast, while English is increasingly popular. However, an attempt at a few basic phrases in Croatian will always be appreciated by the locals, so don't be afraid to use them when the opportunity arises.

Media

In larger cities and resorts, British and other European newspapers and the American *International Herald Tribune* can be found at newsstands and in the big hotel shops. Almost every hotel and even guesthouse seems to have satellite television, and so it's relatively easy to keep up with events around the world through CNN, BBC World Service Television, German and other non-Croatian channels. Croatian television itself broadcasts many US and British programmes in the original language with subtitles in Croatian. Croatian Radio has the news in English each day at 8 a.m., 10 a.m., 2 p.m. and 11 p.m. With a short-wave radio, you can listen to the BBC World Service or Voice of America. It's best to find out the frequencies on which they broadcast before you leave as they change at different times of the day.

91

Money

The Croatian *kuna* (HRK) is divided into 100 *lipa*. Banknotes: 5, 10, 20, 50, 100, 200, 500 and 1,000 kuna. Coins: 10, 20, 50 lipa and 1, 2 and 5 kuna. Credit cards are increasingly accepted in hotels, restaurants and shops, and can also be used for cash advances at banks and exchange offices, though this is an expensive way of obtaining *kuna*. You can also draw cash at most ATM machines with an ordinary cash card, using your regular PIN number. The best solution is probably to take a variety of financial tools: some cash, travellers cheques and a credit card.

Keep the receipt when you buy your Croatian money, as you may need to show it in order to change any remaining *kuna* back again.

Opening Hours

The following times are a general guide and can vary according to region and time of year.

Banks open Monday to Friday 8 a.m.–8 p.m., and Saturday 8 a.m.–1 p.m. Hours may be more flexible in coastal tourist resorts.

Many shops and department stores open from 7.30 or 8 a.m. to 7 or 8 p.m. during the week, and from 8 a.m. to 2 p.m. on Saturday. You may find Mediterranean-length lunch breaks apply along the coast. In the major tourist towns, restaurants will be open all day, seven days a week.

It is best to check the hours of museums before making any special plans to visit, as times can be severely limited. The big museums in Zagreb are usually open throughout the week from around 10 a.m. to 5 p.m. However, in other towns, many close at midday or 1 p.m. To be on the safe side, make sure your museum trips are in the morning.

Public Transport

Air. In such a small country, getting around by plane may seem an undue luxury. But if you are in a hurry, the slow, mountainous drive from Zagreb to Dubrovnik could make you think otherwise. Croatia Airlines has daily internal flights from Zagreb to Pula, Split and Dubrovnik. The ordinary fare is expensive, but there are good reductions for advance bookings, students, seniors and family groups. Further details and other information can be obtained from your local Croatia Airlines office or contact the main office in Zagreb: tel. (385) 1 4872-727; fax (385) 1 4819-633
www.croatiaairlines.com

Intercity Buses. Speedy, frequent and efficient, intercity express buses are the people's choice for travel within Croatia, and routes extend throughout the country. In high season in particular it's advised to book your seat in advance. Luggage is meant to be stowed separately and incurs a supplement per bag.

Train. While they are slower than buses and reach fewer destinations, Croatia's trains are also cheaper and more comfortable, and if you have time to spare they are a pleasant way of travelling. Trains run daily from Zagreb to Osijek, Rijeka and Varaždin, and along a spectacular track via Knin to Zadar and Split. There's usually no problem with finding a seat on local or stopping trains, but it would be wise to reserve your place on an express service.

Ferries. The most relaxing way of all to head south is to take a cabin on one of the large Jadrolinija ferries and cruise along the coast. There are regular sailings from Rijeka to Dubrovnik, calling at Zadar, Split and Hvar, with the daytime part of the 22-hour journey between Split and Dubrovnik the most scenic. You can break your journey at any of the stops as long as you get your ticket validated by the purser. On board you'll find a restaurant and cafeteria. You would be well advised to book your cabin in advance in peak times.

Apart from this service, Jadrolinija's distinctive white-and-blue boats can be seen all around the Adriatic coast providing car- and passenger-crossings between the mainland and the most important islands. If you are taking a car across in summer, make sure you get to the ferry in plenty of time as they operate on a first-come first-served basis.

There are also fast hydrofoils run by private companies that zoom up and down the coast, but these are more expensive. A hydrofoil will whisk you over to Venice in an hour from the Istrian peninsula but they only run till the end of September.

International ferry services sail to Croatia from Italy, with crossings from Ancona to Split and from Bari to Dubrovnik.

Local transport. Zagreb is crisscrossed by a network of distinctive blue-and-white trams. The service is good, though crowded. Make sure you have a ticket (purchased at newspaper kiosks) before you board the tram. If you are staying in the centre of town, you will probably be able to walk to most places of interest. Other major towns such as Osijek, Rijeka, Split and Dubrovnik have inexpensive local bus systems.

Religion

Croatia's Serb population (4.5%) belong to the Eastern Orthodox Church, and there are small Muslim, Jewish and Protestant communities. The vast majority of Croatians, however, are Roman Catholic (88%). As far back as Bishop Gregory of Nin's championing of the Croatian language in the liturgy, the Catholic church was a means of asserting an independent national identity against various foreign rulers (as well as the Communist authorities of the former Yugoslavia).

Security
Croatia has a very low crime rate, and is one of those rare places where you and your belongings will be safe, whether on the back streets of Zagreb or the beaches of the Dalmatian coast. Nevertheless, make sure wallets and handbags are secure and leave your valuables in the hotel safe. You are obliged by the police to carry your passport with you, so keep it in a button-down pocket or bag with zip or clasp.

Time
Croatia is one hour ahead of GMT. When it is noon in Croatia, it is 11 a.m. in London and 6 a.m. in New York. Daylight saving comes into operation in March, when clocks are put forward an hour (GMT + 2).

Tipping
A service charge is usually included in restaurant bills and taxi fares. If the service has been especially good you may want to round off the amount, but there's no obligation to do so.

Toilets
Men's and women's toilets (*zahodi*) are generally marked by a male or female figure, and sometimes by the outline of a man's or woman's shoe. The Croatian for Men is *muški* and Women is *ženski*. There isn't a great profusion of public facilities, so you might find yourself making use of those in cafés or bars, in which case it is probably polite to stop for a drink as well.

Tourist Offices
Most towns have a municipal tourist bureau *(turist biro)*. These are useful for brochures, maps and information about museum opening hours and local events. Private tourist agencies, such as Atlas, Kompas and Kvarner Express are prominently placed in all the main tourist locations and can help in finding private rooms and arranging tours. They also offer exchange facilities.

The Croatian National Tourist Board helpline (062 999 999) operates between 8 a.m. and midnight from mid-June to the end of September.
See also:
   www.croatia.hr
   e-mail: info@htz.hr

I N D E X

INDEX

GENERAL EDITOR:
  Barbara Ender-Jones
STAFF EDITOR:
  Alice Taucher
LAYOUT:
  Luc Malherbe
PHOTO CREDITS
All photos Rainer Hackenberg
except:
  Jonathan Blair/Corbis: p. 1
  Hémisphères/Wysocki: front
  cover, p. 13, 81
  Hémisphères/Frances pp. 69,
  72
  Croatian Tourist Office p. 58
MAPS:
Elsner & Schichor,
Kartographie Huber
JPM Publications

Copyright © 2004
by JPM Publications SA
12, avenue William-Fraisse,
1006 Lausanne, Schweiz
information@jpmguides.com
http://www.jpmguides.com/

Printed in Switzerland
Weber/Bienne (CTP) — 04/06/01
Edition 2004–2005